JOINT WORKING GROUP
BETWEEN THE ROMAN CATHOLIC CHURCH AND THE WORLD COUNCIL OF CHURCHES

EIGHTH REPORT
1999-2005

JOINT WORKING GROUP BETWEEN THE ROMAN CATHOLIC CHURCH AND THE WORLD COUNCIL OF CHURCHES

EIGHTH REPORT
1999-2005

GENEVA-ROME 2005

WCC
Publications
Geneva

Cover design: Rob Lucas

ISBN 2-8254-1427-1

Table of Contents

Foreword

We have been privileged to moderate the Joint Working Group during its eighth mandate. The fruits of its work are the substance of this report.

Though not itself a council, the Joint Working Group has acted as an instrument of the World Council of Churches and the Roman Catholic Church (Pontifical Council for the Promotion of Christian Unity) in promoting the ecumenical movement. Its study entitled "Inspired by the Same Vision" has addressed conciliar developments through-out the world and the impetus given by Catholic participation in national and regional councils of churches. It also speaks from experience in addressing the nature and pur-pose of ecumenical dialogue, the privileged modality of interchurch engagement.

Not forgetful of the goal of the ecumenical movement it has, at the insistence of its parent bodies, examined in depth the ecclesiological and ecumenical implications of a common baptism, and recommends to churches a study of its findings. In baptism and the profession of (baptismal) faith the journey of the Christian and all Christian faith communities begins, a journey which has a common goal in and through Christ Jesus our Lord. To bear united witness to his gospel provokes our ecumenical efforts; our as yet unfinished study on Christian anthropology will cast light on human nature as shaped by grace on which such efforts must be based. This is a study which we believe must continue.

We thank the officers of our respective mandating bodies – the World Council of Churches and the Pontifical Council for the Promotion of Christian Unity – and all the members of our plenary meetings for their generous commitment to the cause of church unity, and recommend to our readers the study of our report.

Rt Rev. Dr Jonas Jonson
Bishop of Stängnäs, Sweden

Most Rev. Mario Conti
Archbishop of Glasgow, UK

Co-Moderators of the Joint Working Group

I. Introduction

The Joint Working Group (JWG) appreciates the importance of the mandate it has received from the Roman Catholic Church and the World Council of Churches to assist in carrying out the ecumenical mission of the churches. In seeking to fulfil our mandate in the period 1999-2005 we are increasingly convinced of the priority that needs to be given to efforts to grow towards the unity that Christ wills for his church.

The year 2004 is the 40th anniversary of the Decree on Ecumenism of the Second Vatican Council (*Unitatis Redintegratio*) and 2005 that of the foundation of the JWG. It is proposed that these anniversaries be marked by a joint consultation between the RCC and the WCC. The JWG also looks forward to the assembly of the WCC in Porto Alegre Brazil, 14-23 February 2006, on the theme "God, in Your Grace, Transform the World".

In the period of our mandate the Group held five plenary meetings: in Antelias (Lebanon 2000), Dromantine (Northern Ireland 2001), Stjärnholm (Sweden 2002), Bari (Italy 2003) and Chania/Crete (Greece 2004). In expressing thanks to those who hosted the meetings, the Group wishes to acknowledge the hospitality of the local churches that shared their lives, their struggles, their traditions and their ecumenical experiences with us.

The period 1999-2005 began in the anticipation of the Jubilee of the year 2000 and the hopes awakened by the celebrations of two millennia of Christian history. Many of those hopes are bearing fruit, but the period has also been marked by difficult and tragic situations for the world and by new challenges for the churches.

This report outlines the activities of the JWG during these years and includes three completed study documents, as well as some themes pursued and issues addressed.

Among the most valuable aspects of our work has been the Christian fellowship we have experienced, the sharing that has been possible of information from every part of the world, and the growth in communion and understanding that has taken place among us.

II. Relationships 1999-2005

1. Significant moments: bilateral visits; leadership meetings

During the period under review, there have been several significant moments in the bilateral relations between the World Council of Churches and the Pontifical Council for Promoting Christian Unity. Bishop Walter Kasper, then secretary of the PCPCU, paid his first official visit to the WCC (31 January-1 February 2000). The purpose of the visit was threefold:

- to get to know the WCC and its programmes;
- to meet the staff leadership group and other members of the WCC staff; and
- to evaluate the state of the relations between the two partners.

One session with the PCPCU delegation focused on three aspects:

1) a review of plans for the JWG plenary foreseen that year in May;
2) the participation of the RCC in WCC programmes without being a member of the WCC (except in Faith and Order, and Mission and Evangelism) and participation or full membership in councils of churches at local and regional level;
3) the changing ecumenical configuration whereby churches find themselves in a new situation with Pentecostals and Evangelicals being among the fastest growing communities and yet the large majority of them still outside the WCC and the ecumenical movement.

There was consensus in this free discussion that there was a need to assess the impact of the changing situation on the ecumenical movement. In this context, several questions emerged for further reflection and discussion by both sides:

1) Could the WCC and the RCC think of a consultation where all possible partners would come together and exchange their ideas on the changing shape of the ecumenical movement?
2) What role would Christian world communions (CWCs) play in such a consultation?
3) What kind of an agenda would be discussed at such a consultation?

The second significant moment in the relations between the two partners was the leadership meeting that took place on 31 May 2000 in Antelias, Lebanon, on the occasion of the JWG plenary, 25-31 May 2000, hosted by Catholicos Aram I. Present at the meeting were, from the WCC, Catholicos Aram I (moderator of the WCC central committee), Rev. Dr Konrad Raiser (WCC general secretary) and Bishop Jonas Jonson (co-moderator of the JWG); from the RCC, Cardinal Edward Cassidy (president of the PCPCU), Bishop Walter Kasper (then secretary of the PCPCU) and Bishop Mario Conti (co-moderator of the JWG). The meeting was also attended by staff members on both sides.

The issues discussed on this occasion included the following: a brief evaluation of the JWG plenary in Antelias; information on future priorities of the JWG and methodology; a sharing of ideas on WCC-RCC collaboration through Faith and Order; WCC-RCC collaboration on mission and evangelism; and issues of collaboration in the coming years.

The second leadership meeting also took place in Antelias, Lebanon, on 4 March 2004, hosted by Catholicos Aram I, on the occasion of the meeting of the JWG executive 4-7 March 2004. The leadership meeting was convened following the election of the new WCC general secretary, Rev. Dr Samuel Kobia. The meeting took place in three phases. Catholicos Aram I met with Cardinal Walter Kasper, they were then joined by Dr Samuel Kobia and Bishop Brian Farrell, and finally the leadership group met with all members of the JWG executive.

The agenda discussed at this leadership meeting included issues such as: the possibility of RCC membership in the WCC under the category of "churches in association with the WCC"; mutual invitation to one another's major events; proper procedures for communication between departments of the WCC and the Roman Curia; and the mandate of the JWG. Attention was drawn to the fact that the JWG would be celebrating its 40th anniversary in 2005. The leadership meeting accepted a proposal that on the occasion of that anniversary, the two partners could convene a consultation that would evaluate the relationship between the RCC and the WCC.

During this period, the WCC received Bishop Marc Ouellet (then secretary of the PCPCU) on his first official visit to the WCC on 25 October 2001. A similar visit by Bishop Brian Farrell (secretary of the PCPCU) took place on 1 April 2003. Both visits were mutually arranged for the purpose of getting to know the WCC, its programmes and staff, as well as some of the issues in which the two partners are engaged.

The PCPCU received the staff team of Mission and Evangelism on its visit to Rome, 19-24 October 2001. The programme, organized by the PCPCU, involved participation in the general audience of Pope John Paul II, and contacts with the offices of the Roman Curia that have relationship with programmes of CWME, the faculty of missiology at the Urbaniana Pontifical University, the Union of Superiors General (women religious) and the SEDOS Centre for Documentation.

From 4 to 7 December 2003, a delegation of 12 persons representing various offices of the Roman Curia, some faculties of theology, religious men and women and the Centre for Documentation, visited the WCC at the invitation of the staff working on the programme on Mission and Evangelism. The purpose of the visit was mainly to receive information from the WCC on the conference on world mission and evangelism, to be held in Athens 9-16 May 2005 under the theme "Come, Holy Spirit, Heal and

Reconcile!". Besides an introduction to the WCC for the delegation, some of whom were visiting the WCC for the first time, the programme included an exposure to the theme of the conference and concluded with a morning of prayerful retreat in the style of *lectio divina*. In connection with the CWME conference in Athens, the PCPCU has already received an invitation from the WCC to send a delegation.

2. Celebration of the Jubilee 2000

In its seventh report (1998), the JWG highlighted the ecumenical potential of the celebration of the Jubilee Year 2000. The preparation required continuous dialogue with ecumenical partners through the "Ecumenical Commission of the Central Committee of the Great Jubilee". Besides other ecumenical partners, the WCC was represented on this commission by a fraternal delegate (Mr Georges Lemopoulos, deputy general secretary) 1996-99. Three WCC delegates (Bishop Jonas Jonson, Rev. Dr Alan Falconer, director of Faith and Order, and Ms Teny Pirri-Simonian, co-secretary of the JWG) were among the 23 fraternal delegates that attended the opening of the Holy Door by Pope John Paul II, at the Basilica of St Paul Outside the Walls on 18 January 2000. It was the first time in history that such a Jubilee liturgical event took place in an ecumenical service.

Another Jubilee event at which a fraternal delegate represented the WCC was the "Ecumenical Commemoration of Witnesses to the Faith in the Twentieth Century", on 7 May 2000 at the Colosseum in Rome. Pope John Paul II reflected on this event earlier when he said, "The greatest homage which all the churches can give to Christ on the threshold of the third millennium will be to manifest the fruits of faith, hope and charity present in men and women of many different tongues and races who have followed Christ" (*Tertio Millennio Adveniente* (TMA), 37).

A third important event during the Jubilee year was the celebration entitled "Ecumenical Witness as the Third Millennium Begins". Pope John Paul II led this ecumenical celebration of the word on 25 January 2001, at the Basilica of St Paul Outside the Walls, together with representatives of other churches, Christian world communions and the WCC, represented by Bishop Jonas Jonson (co-moderator, JWG) and Rev. Dr Alan Falconer (director of Faith and Order). As described by Pope John Paul II, the purpose of the celebration was to demonstrate the determination of Christians to embark upon the new millennium in a spirit of reconciliation, providing an atmosphere of heartfelt prayer that the Holy Spirit may grant the gift of visible unity to Christ's followers (cf. presentation for the Week of Prayer for Christian Unity Celebration at St Paul's Outside the Walls, 25 January 2001).

The calendar of the Jubilee of the Catholic Church included a "prayer vigil in response to the appeal of the patriarch of Constantinople" on the evening of 5 August 2000. In this event the Catholic Church accepted the 1996 appeal of the Ecumenical Patriarch Bartholomew I that all Christians promote a common spirit of doxology and invocation on the eve of the Solemn Feast of the Transfiguration of Our Lord.

Throughout the Jubilee year representatives of other churches were invited to send fraternal delegates to other events such as a jubilee event for journalists, a meeting of university teachers and the World Congress of Catholic Laity. The ecumenical patriarch organized an international Orthodox youth assembly in Istanbul, Turkey, in June 2000, at which a delegation of ten young Catholics, representing various youth organizations, took part. At the World Youth Day in August 2000, ecumenical prayers were organized every evening. Important ecumenical events also took place at local levels. It is worth remembering, for example, the common celebration of all the churches present in the Holy Land and Jerusalem.

3. Assisi World Day of Prayer for Peace

Threats to peace and justice in the world have continued and in many ways intensified during the period of the JWG mandate. Pope John Paul II convened the Assisi World Day of Prayer for Peace on 24 January 2002, mainly in response to the build-up of tensions following the tragic events of 11 September 2001. The pope invited the leaders of various churches, representatives of Christian world communions and the WCC, as well as leaders of other world religions, to a day of prayer for peace in Assisi. Catholic bishops from different regions of the world participated in the event. The WCC was represented by the Rev. Dr Konrad Raiser who read the first of ten commitments to peace.

The Day of Prayer for Peace of 24 January 2002, like the two previous ones in Assisi, was both ecumenical and inter-religious, and thus only the opening of the event and its conclusion were done together, leaving a moment of prayer for each religious group to pray in a different place according to its own faith, language, tradition, and with full respect for others. What bound together all participants in Assisi was the certainty that peace is a gift of God, for each person is called to be a peace-maker. The event was all the more interesting due to the fact that it included a pilgrimage by train, carrying the pope and all specially invited delegates to Assisi and back together.

4. The one ecumenical movement: questions of "reconfiguration"

From 1991 to 1998 the WCC concentrated its attention on a reflection process entitled "Towards a Common Understanding and Vision of the WCC" (CUV). The RCC offered a substantial contribution that was taken into consideration when drafting the policy statement which ensued. The process known as "the reconfiguration of the one ecumenical movement" has been one of three direct results of the policy document, also entitled "Towards a Common Understanding and Vision of the WCC". A second one was the exploration of a global Christian forum (see point 6) to address the issue of widening the fellowship of churches to include Evangelical, Pentecostal and Independent churches, as well as the Roman Catholic Church, and the other churches and organizations which have traditionally been part of the ecumenical movement. The third result was the Special Commission on Orthodox Participation in the WCC (see point 5), which dealt mainly with issues internal to the fellowship of the member churches of the WCC and became the place for a sustained reflection on models for a possible restructuring of the Council itself.

Discussions about a possible new reconfiguration of the ecumenical movement have started in meetings between various ecumenical partners such as the regional ecumenical organizations (REOs), national councils of churches (NCCs), Christian world communions (CWCs) and ecumenical agencies. The general secretary of the WCC brought the matter to the attention of the central committee and the decision was taken to initiate a process of consultation in order to address the question of how relationships can be strengthened between existing ecumenical actors.

A first meeting took place in Antelias, Lebanon, 12-17 November 2003, with the participation of a staff member of the PCPCU. A report entitled "From Antelias with Love" was issued and sent to WCC member churches, the PCPCU and other ecumenical partners for discussion and response. It suggested some next steps and affirmed the need for the WCC to "consult with other churches who are part of the ecumenical movement, such as the Roman Catholic Church" and to "encourage their participation in discussions of reconfiguration". A second meeting was held at the end of 2004. There are some conceptual difficulties which need to be considered in this process. Thus it is proposed to continue the exploration of a "reconfiguration" within a general perspective on "the one ecumenical movement in the 21st century".

5.   Special Commission on Orthodox Participation in the WCC

The Special Commission on Orthodox Participation in the WCC was inaugurated at the WCC's eighth assembly in Harare, Zimbabwe, in 1998, because of serious concerns about aspects of the functioning of the WCC expressed among Orthodox churches. Furthermore, the assembly noted that other churches and ecclesial families had concerns similar to those expressed by the Orthodox. The Special Commission has been unique in WCC history in being composed of an equal number of representatives from Orthodox churches and from the other member churches of the WCC.

The commission fulfilled its twofold task: "to study and analyze the whole spectrum of issues related to Orthodox participation in the WCC" and "to make proposals [to the WCC central committee] concerning the necessary changes in structure, style and ethos of the Council". Its report was presented to the central committee in 2002, making concrete proposals in five areas: (1) membership, including the creation of a new possible place for "churches in association with the fellowship of the WCC"; (2) consensus decision-making; (3) ecclesiology; (4) ethical and social matters, and (5) common prayer. A steering committee was set up and mandated to continue work in these areas until the ninth assembly of the WCC, when a final report will be presented. Some of the constitutional and institutional changes proposed by the commission which will have to be considered by the assembly include: (1) the addition of theological criteria to the "criteria of membership"; (2) churches becoming members of the fellowship after a probation period; and (3) new rules of debate, according to the consensus method. The statement on ecclesiology prepared by Faith and Order for the next assembly has largely covered the ecclesiological concerns expressed by the Special Commission.

The Joint Working Group received regular reports on the work of the Special Commission as the RCC is interested in relationships with Orthodox churches, on the one hand, and in institutional developments in the WCC, on the other.

6.   Global Christian forum

In the context of the exploration in the 1990s of a "Common Understanding and Vision of the WCC" (see JWG seventh report, III A.5), the general secretary, Rev. Dr Konrad Raiser, raised the question of whether there was need for an "ad hoc ecumenical forum of Christian churches and ecumenical organizations" in which various partners could come together in a new way, with the WCC being one participant among them. It would also include those Evangelicals and Pentecostals whose communities are growing and have not been involved in the organized ecumenical movement.

During 1997-98, the WCC invited the PCPCU to explore the feasibility of this idea with representatives of other churches and ecumenical organizations. The PCPCU accepted the invitation, with the following understanding: that priority should be given first to settling the reorganization of the WCC outlined in the CUV policy statement; that the forum should be a channel for strengthening the goal of visible unity which is stated in the constitution of the WCC, even if this goal was not expressly stated in the purposes of the proposed forum; and that it should meet a need not being met by any existing organization. The PCPCU expressed the hope that a proposed forum could serve as an occasion to draw into the one ecumenical movement those many Christians who presently seem to steer clear of the ecumenical movement in its more organized forms.

A first consultation was convened by the WCC in August 1998. Noting the diversity of efforts to advance Christian unity, the participants felt a forum was *possible* because of the unity already given in Christ and was *called for* because of our common faith in a reconciling God. A preliminary proposal was drawn up and a continuation committee was appointed with the task to explore the idea further. From the beginning a PCPCU staff person has taken part in the committee. To underline that this is a common search and not a project of the WCC or any other organization or church, the committee is considered autonomous.

The first step taken by the continuation committee was to test the proposal with those who thus far had not been so involved in the organized forms of the ecumenical movement. Thus some twenty leaders from Evangelical and Pentecostal churches responded to an invitation to a meeting which was held in September 2000 at Fuller Theological Seminary, Pasadena, USA. The group responded positively to the idea, which they named a "global Christian forum". They agreed that the forum should focus on the mission of the church and that the purpose should be to foster common witness.

The positive response from the preliminary testing of the idea encouraged the continuation committee to organize a further event in June 2002, also at Fuller Theological Seminary. Some sixty participants from Orthodox, Catholic, Protestant, Anglican, Evangelical, Pentecostal, Holiness and African Instituted churches and from international Christian organizations were brought together. It was the first time that such a broadly representative group of all the main traditions of Christianity in the world today met to discuss the forum proposal. The meeting affirmed the proposal and formulated a provisional purpose statement. It affirmed that the forum should hold together mission and unity, and underlined the value of the process of bringing Christians and churches together. It also expanded the continuation committee. Afterwards, a plan was devised covering the years 2004-2007.

7. *Koinonia*: central to the ecumenical movement

During the period under review, 1999-2005, both the WCC and the PCPCU focused attention on the question of the unity of the church expressed as *communio/koinonia* and on the nature of the fellowship of churches in the WCC within the one ecumenical movement. Catholicos Aram I, in his report as moderator of the WCC central committee in

1999, dealt with the issue of the fellowship of churches in the context of the WCC eighth assembly in Harare and the study process on "A Common Understanding and Vision of the WCC", which "sought not only to clarify a vision for the WCC, but also to elucidate the nature of the fellowship of churches in the WCC".

At the WCC central committee of August-September 1999, the moderator underlined the centrality of ecclesiology in speaking about both the WCC fellowship of churches and the ecumenical movement in general. The report of the central committee described fellowship in terms of mutuality: mutual vision, mutual respect, mutual love, mutual understanding, mutual correction, mutual challenge and mutual accountability. From the principle of mutuality, the report underlined the specific identity of the WCC that creates a sense of togetherness among member churches: a fellowship of churches with an inclusive vision, open to sharing the drama of a broken world. The fellowship of churches has a vocation to reach out beyond its borders in a situation of globalization marked by increasing interdependence and growing pluralism. The report thus called for collaboration with regional and national councils of churches in a spirit of mutual respect and trust. It also urged the Council to develop this vision of a fellowship that is open to all churches, beyond present institutional boundaries, leading them together towards the full and visible unity of the church.

The PCPCU from 2001 onwards considered not only the present state of the journey of churches towards Christian unity, but also the need to clarify a vision of ecumenism from the RCC perspective.

At its plenary of November 2001, Cardinal Walter Kasper, the president of the PCPCU, spoke of communion as the guiding concept of Catholic ecumenical theology. In his address he noted that in the bilateral dialogues in which the Catholic church has been engaged over 35 years the central concept is that of *communio*. It is indeed the key concept for all bilateral and multilateral dialogues. The theological foundations of this concept of *communio* can be traced to the New Testament where, for example, in the Acts of the Apostles, the early church in Jerusalem constituted a *koinonia* in the breaking of bread and in prayer (Acts 2:44, 4:33). *Koinonia* is also a central theme in the Johannine and Pauline epistles. The Cardinal also observed that the Second Vatican Council adopted this *communio* ecclesiology (LG 3, 7, 11, 23, 26; UR 2) that contains both a vertical sacramental view and a horizontal communal perspective. The Second Vatican Council considers ecclesial *communio* to be based on, and prefigured in the Trinitarian communion of Father, Son and Holy Spirit (LG 4; UR 2), a model of *communio* that is constitutive of the church. The president of the PCPCU observed that even though we may speak of a far-reaching ecumenical convergence on the concept of communion, it was clear that a firm ecumenical consensus was still far away, given the different ecclesiologies that are still operative among dialogue partners.

III. Collaboration between the RCC and the WCC

The JWG oversees and seeks to foster not only ad hoc relationships which allow the RCC and the WCC to address together specific issues of mutual concern, but also to encourage the establishment of institutional links between programmes and teams of the WCC and the Vatican whereby the partners can formally collaborate in the wide range of issues being addressed by both.

1. Faith and Order

Even though the RCC is not a member of the WCC, it is fully represented with 12 members, drawn from different regions of the world, on the commission on Faith and Order.

Since the Harare assembly in 1998, major studies of the Faith and Order commission have focused on: the nature and purpose of the church; baptism; ecumenical hermeneutics; theological anthropology; ethnic identity, national identity and the search for unity; worship; and (since 2002) theological reflection on peace. The secretariat has also been involved in supporting United-Uniting churches, at their request, through a biannual survey of church union negotiations and through the organization of a conference in Driebergen in 2002 for these churches. It has also responded to the request of the Conference of Secretaries of Christian World Communions to bring together those involved in bilateral dialogues in the bilateral forum to consider issues of common concern. The last of these took place in 2001. The secretariat published a collection of all international bilateral dialogues 1982-98 – *Growth in Agreement II* (Faith and Order paper 187, 2000).

The work on ecclesiology has involved a number of facets. The commission has been engaged in re-drafting the nature and purpose of the church in light of some 45 responses from churches, councils of churches and theological institutes. A major contribution was submitted by a group of Roman Catholic theologians convened by Cardinal Kasper, president of PCPCU, while another came from the archdiocese of Toronto. Moreover, a series of consultations have been held on ecclesiology : "Does the Church Have a Sacramental Nature?", "Authority and Authoritative Teaching", and

"Ministry and Ordination in the Community of Women and Men and the Church". A consultation was also held on "Ecclesiology and Mission", co-sponsored with the commission on World Mission and Evangelism. The papers and reports from these consultations are in process of publication. The commission has also been invited to prepare a statement on ecclesiology: "The Church: Local and Universal, One and Diverse" for the WCC's ninth assembly.

During this period, the secretariat has been involved in a number of collaborative ventures, leading to the presentation to central committee and subsequent publication of a statement "A Church of All and for All" with the Ecumenical Disability Advocates Network, and a discussion paper with Mission and Evangelism and Inter-religious Dialogue teams on "A Theology of Religious Plurality".

2. Mission and Evangelism

The PCPCU continues to support and facilitate collaboration with the work of the WCC staff team responsible for mission and evangelism, as well as for health and healing, community and justice, and education and ecumenical formation. This is demonstrated significantly through the continued appointment of a full-time Roman Catholic consultant to work with the WCC staff team in these programme areas. During this mandate of the JWG, the person holding this appointment has been Sister Elizabeth Moran of the Missionary Sisters of Saint Columban.

During this mandate of the JWG there have been changes in personnel and organizational structure in the WCC staffing of this work. The Roman Catholic consultant was asked by the WCC to play a key part in the reorganization, and with the full support and approval of the PCPCU undertook the role of interim coordinator of the staff team during this period of realignment, which led to a new team on Mission and Ecumenical Formation. This interim assignment bears witness to the maturity of the partnership between the WCC and the RCC, in that the WCC could invite a consultant from a non-WCC member church to undertake such a key role, and that the RCC could commit itself to sharing its gifts and expertise in such a way with a partner organization.

Some additional appointments of Catholics to WCC bodies have brought a new dimension to the spectrum of cooperation and liaison between the WCC and the RCC. The new by-laws of the commission on World Mission and Evangelism (CWME) provide for the presence of three Roman Catholic members. The PCPCU has appointed three full members of the 30-person commission that advises the Geneva staff on mission concerns. There is also provision for the presence of one Roman Catholic member in the advisory body for Education and Ecumenical Formation and the PCPCU has appointed a religious sister.

A warm invitation has been offered by the WCC to the RCC to participate in the next world mission conference planned for May 2005 in Athens. An equally warm response from the PCPCU has led to a series of meetings to cooperate in preparing this important meeting. The conference theme is "Come, Holy Spirit, Heal and Reconcile!". Such joint preparation is enhancing collaboration between the WCC and the RCC in this significant global gathering that will focus on healing and reconciliation in our world.

Access to resources in the field of mission continues to be facilitated through visits and consultations between the WCC staff and the offices of the Secretary for Education and Documentation Service (SEDOS), the Union of Women's Religious Institutes (UISG) and the Union of Men's Religious Institutes (USG), as well as with several dicasteries of the Roman Curia. WCC representatives have been routinely invited to conferences and meetings organized by the RCC in Rome. Particularly noteworthy was the visit of Geneva staff to Rome in October 2001, which included attendance at the Wednesday public audience with Pope John Paul II, followed by a personal meeting with the Holy Father. In November 2002 the coordinator of the WCC team on Mission, Evangelism and Ecumenical Formation (Rev. Dr Carlos Ham) accompanied by the Roman Catholic consultant (Sr Elizabeth Moran) visited the offices of the Congregation for the Evangelization of Peoples and had a fruitful exchange of information with Archbishop Robert Sarah, secretary of the Congregation, and members of the staff.

Collaboration has been ongoing in the field of health and healing. A particular area of growing dialogue and collaboration is seen in the relations between the WCC and the Pontifical Council for Health Pastoral Care. WCC staff members have been welcomed as participants in the annual international conference organized by the Pontifical Council for Health Pastoral Care. There has been cooperation between the WCC and the RCC in shared work at the World Health Organization and during the world health assembly. On both regional and global levels, the WCC and the Catholic Church have collaborated in the development of the Ecumenical Pharmaceutical Network. Particular note must be made of the cooperation in the event of the major inter-religious consultation "Strategies to Increase Access to HIV/AIDS Prevention, Care and Treatment through Closer Cooperation between Faith-based Organizations and International Organizations" in Nairobi (7-10 May 2003), jointly convened by the WCC, Caritas International and the World Conference on Religion and Peace, and hosted by the All Africa Conference of Churches. This conference laid the ground for new partnerships between faith-based organizations, UN organizations, and internationally operating organizations. These partnerships are intended to assist development of new international initiatives to increase access to prevention, care and treatment for HIV/AIDS.

3.   Ecumenical Formation

The JWG has over the years expressed concern for ecumenical formation and education as fundamental to the search for the unity of the church. In the last mandate, the JWG published a study document entitled "Ecumenical Formation: Ecumenical Reflections and Suggestions". During the present mandate, the JWG has continuously encouraged efforts of ongoing ecumenical formation at the WCC Ecumenical Institute of Bossey, the WCC programme on Education and Ecumenical Formation (EEF) and the WCC programme on Ecumenical Theological Education (ETE).

3.1. ECUMENICAL INSTITUTE OF BOSSEY

In its commitment to the work of ecumenical formation at Bossey, the PCPCU appoints a full-time Catholic professor on the staff of the Institute. Currently Father Gosbert Byamungu occupies that post and accompanies the students each year in their visit to Rome. The PCPCU is also represented on the Bossey board by one of its staff in the capacity of observer. In 2003, Bossey and the PCPCU co-sponsored a major seminar on the "Nature and Purpose of the Ecumenical Movement" at which a paper by

Cardinal Walter Kasper with the same title was read on his behalf by a member of the PCPCU. In 2003, Bossey invited Msgr Frank Dewane of the Pontifical Council for Justice and Peace to give a lecture on issues of justice and peace.

The JWG encourages collaboration between the WCC and the RCC on several aspects of the work of the Ecumenical Institute of Bossey. In the first place, the PCPCU, through its committee for cultural collaboration, offers two full scholarships each year to Bossey for two Orthodox students. Secondly, the PCPCU organizes and sponsors the annual visit to Rome by the students and staff of the Institute. The purpose of the one-week programme in Rome is mainly to offer an opportunity to the students to get to know the Catholic Church from the perspective of its highest offices in order to overcome stereotypes and allow each to get to know the other better. Thus the programme includes an audience with the Holy Father, visits to various offices of the Roman Curia, encounters with representatives of men's and women's religious orders and with Catholic lay movements with ecumenical participation such as the Focolare movement and the St Egidio community. Other aspects of the programme include visits to some faculties of theology and guided tours to important places of Christian history. In recent years, some Catholic students have also participated in the Bossey programme.

The PCPCU considers the role of Bossey in ecumenical formation and education of church leaders as an important contribution to the journey towards Christian unity. The publication by Bossey of "Fifty Years of Ecumenical Formation at the Ecumenical Institute of Bossey: 1952-2002" bears witness to its important contribution over the years.

3.2. EDUCATION AND ECUMENICAL FORMATION (EEF)

The WCC also has a programme on Education and Ecumenical Formation (EEF) geared to help member churches of the WCC. The PCPCU collaborates in that programme by appointing a Catholic consultant as an observer to the EEF working group.

3.3. ECUMENICAL THEOLOGICAL EDUCATION (ETE)

Over the years, the WCC programme on Ecumenical Theological Education (ETE) has worked closely with the RCC directly and indirectly. Father Fred Bliss, a professor of ecumenism at the St Thomas Aquinas Pontifical University in Rome, has been appointed by the PCPCU as consultant to the ETE working group. The PCPCU has suggested Catholic experts for meetings of ETE. The interactive study process on theological education and ministerial formation in Africa in 2001-2002 culminated with a conference in Johannesburg, South Africa, in September 2002, on the theme "The Journey of Hope in Africa Continued". On that occasion the PCPCU proposed both Catholic theological educators and others active in the ecumenical movement in Africa, especially in theological associations, to attend the conference.

3.4. WCC YOUTH INTERNSHIP PROGRAMME

The WCC youth internship programme provides ecumenical learning to young people between 18 and 30 years, seeking to equip them for deeper involvement in the ecumenical movement, and to aid networking among ecumenical youth movements. The networking has been strengthened since 2001, with study visits to Rome included in the yearly programme. Groups of interns have visited Rome in 2001, 2002 and 2004.

The main objectives of the study visits to Rome are to familiarize the interns with the cooperation between the RCC and the WCC and to equip them to strengthen ecumenical relations with the RCC in their countries.

With the support of the JWG, preparations for the visits begin with orientation by WCC staff with explanations of current relations between the WCC and the RCC. The PCPCU organizes and hosts the programme in Rome. Whenever feasible these visits have been scheduled around the meeting of the executive group of the JWG. This has also allowed the interns to attend some of those sessions and learn directly from the work of the JWG.

The programme organized by the PCPCU normally includes, besides participating in the general audience of the Holy Father, visits to a number of Roman Curia offices, Catholic movements such as the Focolare and the St Egidio community as well as the Centro Pro Unione. In addition the group has had guided tours of historical places related to the Christian tradition. The programme has also included a visit to the faculty of theology of the Waldensian church, a WCC member church in Italy.

Each part of the programme has included a time for presentation followed by time for questions and comments. In addition to all the knowledge and information shared, the spiritual life of the Catholic Church, as experienced in the meetings together with the aforementioned lay movements, has been very much appreciated by the interns. Some of them have followed up on the contacts made in Rome by getting to know local Focolare and St Egidio communities in their home countries after the end of their internships. All interns have highlighted the study visits to Rome as a remarkable learning experience which broadens and deepens their understanding of the RCC. The visits to Rome have also provided the interns with an opportunity to strengthen the bonds of friendship and care within their own community. Participation by additional Roman Catholic interns would be welcomed.

4. Inter-religious dialogue

Continuing exchange and cooperation have for a long time characterized the relationship between staff of the Pontifical Council for Interreligious Dialogue (PCID) and the WCC Office on Interreligious Relations and Dialogue (IRRD). This positive relationship has also been characteristic of the time between the eighth and ninth assemblies of the WCC. Yearly joint staff meetings alternating between the Vatican and Geneva have generally involved the entire staff, providing an opportunity for mutual information and exchange as well as for evaluation of ongoing projects and planning for upcoming projects. These staff meetings, unique in the relationship between the WCC and the Vatican, offer a possibility to reflect together on issues of common concern and where possible address them through common projects.

Staff members from the PCID and the IRRD are regularly invited to attend and contribute to meetings organized by the other office, e.g. the PCID assembly, the IRRD dialogue advisory group, as well as other consultations.

Highlights include the following:

1. Since 11 September 2001, inter-religious initiatives at the local, national and international levels have mushroomed and there is a need to keep abreast of

developments as well as to engage in mutual consultation on inter-religious relations. The joint meetings enable staff to respond better to initiatives and to provide a foundation for a common approach or policy.

2. Throughout the period 1999-2005 there has been a mutual exchange on relations with Muslim organizations and an ongoing assessment of the status of Christian-Muslim relations.

3. The PCID and the IRRD have been reflecting on how to relate to the worsening situation between Christians and Hindus in India where concerns have been expressed by Hindus regarding proselytism, and where anti-conversion laws are in place in some Indian states. Given the sensitivities of perceiving an initiative by the PCID-IRRD as undue interference, plans are evolving to address conversion as a general issue in inter-religious relations and dialogue.

4. Building upon the common study project on inter-religious prayer in the mid-1990s (cf. special issues of *Pro Dialogo* and *Current Dialogue*), preparations are under way to address together emerging theological questions evolving in relation to inter-religious prayer.

5. A common initiative was launched to focus on the contributions of Africa to the religious and spiritual heritage in the world. This project is an attempt to provide space for various aspects of African religiosity and culture to be explored as a constructive and resourceful contribution to a world of religious plurality. This focus should not only give visibility to problems in Africa but also to the many and deeply spiritual contributions provided by the manifold expressions of religion on the continent and in the African diaspora. The project has so far seen three meetings: in Enugu, Nigeria (January 2001); Dakar, Senegal (December 2002); and Addis Ababa, Ethiopia (September 2004). These meetings brought together representatives of Christianity in Africa, representatives of Islam, and followers of African Traditional Religion, as well as representatives of some of the various religious communities of Africa in the diaspora. The theme focused on the family as a source of values and spirituality. A concluding publication of the findings is available.

5. Bilateral and multilateral dialogue

The importance of multilateral dialogue has been effectively illustrated by the fact that the Faith and Order convergence text *Baptism, Eucharist and Ministry* (BEM) has contributed significantly in various ways to reconciliation and/or new relationships between separated churches. The RCC cooperates with the WCC in multilateral dialogue as a full member of the Faith and Order commission, and by participating in Faith and Order's broad range of studies. When Cardinal Kasper met with Catholicos Aram I and the Rev. Dr Samuel Kobia at Antelias in 2004, he emphasized the importance of this work as a priority for the continuing collaboration of the RCC with the WCC.

Bilateral dialogues are important because they permit two Christian churches or communions to face together issues directly related to the particular division they have experienced with each other. Many WCC member churches such as the Orthodox or Oriental Orthodox churches are engaged in bilateral dialogue with the Roman Catholic Church. Others are involved in these dialogues or consultations on the national level, and especially on the international level through their Christian world communion, including Lutherans, Anglicans, Methodists, Reformed, Disciples of Christ, Mennonites, Baptists and Pentecostals. The 1999 signing of the Joint Declaration on the Doctrine of Justification by the Roman Catholic Church and the Lutheran World Federation was a particular achievement in which Lutheran member churches of the WCC took part.

The secretary of the PCPCU and officials of the WCC participate in the annual meetings of the conference of secretaries of the Christian world communions (CWCs). This informal body has periodically sponsored a forum on bilateral dialogues to monitor developments in bilateral dialogues and foster the coherence between bilateral and multilateral dialogue within the one ecumenical movement. The CWCs ask Faith and Order to convene this bilateral forum on its behalf. The eighth forum's theme was "The Implications of Regional Bilateral Agreements for the International Dialogues of Christian World Communions" (2001). One aspect of its report illustrated briefly the way in which the results of both bilateral and multilateral dialogue are being received through formal agreements instituting changed relationships. The report also noted the difficulty of reception of the results of bilateral dialogues because of asymmetrical structures for reception, while at the same time noting that some communions have developed structures precisely to further reception processes.

6.   Week of Prayer for Christian Unity

Since 1966 the WCC Faith and Order commission and the PCPCU have collaborated annually in preparing the materials used ecumenically during the Week of Prayer for Christian Unity, and on other occasions. This long-standing cooperative project between the RCC and the WCC offers each year materials for prayer and biblical reflection on the theme of Christian unity. Both parties believe that such prayer and reflection is the very basis of the search for Christian unity.

Faith and Order and the PCPCU continued this close collaboration on the Week of Prayer for Christian Unity during the period of the present mandate of the JWG. The parties alternate in identifying a local ecumenical group to produce a draft set of materials, and in making arrangements for the international preparatory meeting at which these local draft texts are revised for international distribution. Several of the themes from recent years have found a special echo among the churches and communities: for example the 2004 theme of peace, with material produced by local ecumenical partners in Aleppo, Syria.

In a series of meetings, starting from an intensive brainstorming at Los Rubios, Spain, in 2001, the preparatory group has reflected on the process of the Week of Prayer materials from initial preparation to production and use. The central concern continues to be the relation between a local group responsible for the initial draft material and the international preparatory group whose role is to advise and revise.

With the Week of Prayer materials for 2005, an important advance is noted: the WCC Faith and Order commission and the PCPCU have moved beyond joint preparation and parallel publication to formal *joint publication* of the materials, now in a common format.

Topics of the Weeks of Prayer for 2000-2005 and the location of the initial preparatory group are as follows:

2000: *Blessed be God who has blessed us in Christ* (Eph. 1:3-14), preparatory material, Middle East Council of Churches; meeting at La Verna, Italy

2001: *I am the Way, and the Truth, and the Life* (John 14:1-6), preparatory material, Romania; meeting at Vulcan, Romania

2002: *For with you is the fountain of life* (Ps. 36:5-9), preparatory material, Concilium Conferentiarum Episcoporum Europae and the Conference of European Churches; meeting near Augsburg, Germany

2003: *We have this treasure in clay jars* (2 Cor. 4:4-18), preparatory material from Argentina; meeting at Los Rubios, Spain

2004: *My peace I give to you* (John 14:23-31), preparatory material from Aleppo; meeting in Palermo, Italy

2005: *Christ, the one foundation of the church* (1 Cor. 3:1-23), preparatory material and meeting, Slovak Republic

IV. Collaboration through the JWG

1. Character and nature of the JWG

The JWG was set up in May 1965 by mutual agreement between the WCC and the RCC as an instrument of collaboration between the two partners. Its purpose, described in 1966, was "to explore possibilities of dialogue and collaboration, to study problems jointly, and to report to the competent authorities of either side". In the seventh report, the JWG was described as a consultative forum that "has no authority in itself but reports to its parent bodies – the WCC assembly and the central committee, and the PCPCU". Thus the JWG has an advisory function and serves as an instrument for promoting cooperation between the RCC and the WCC. The JWG receives its mandate every seven years from its parent bodies – the WCC assembly and the PCPCU. At the end of each mandate, the JWG prepares and submits to its parent bodies a detailed report on its activities. This report is examined by the parent bodies who offer their observations and approval and give further guidelines for the next mandate.

During this term, each parent body appointed 17 members to the JWG, selected from different regions of the world, with varied pastoral and ecumenical experiences. The JWG meets in plenary once a year led by two co-moderators. The co-moderators, the co-secretaries and two corresponding staff persons form an executive that meets twice a year. The executive oversees the work of the JWG between its plenaries and prepares the agenda and materials for them.

As stated in the seventh report, the JWG "initiates, evaluates and sustains forms of collaboration between the WCC and the RCC, especially between the various organs and programmes of the WCC and the RCC". The structure and style of the JWG is meant to be flexible and adaptable to the changing needs and priorities of the JWG agenda. The JWG thus sets up sub-commissions to study specific topics on its agenda. Some topics may require the participation of experts from outside the group who may contribute to the ongoing study. The JWG has among its tasks the function of initiating and helping to keep alive the discussion, in the member churches of the WCC and the RCC, of issues facing the ecumenical movement. It also assesses the current trends in the ecumenical movement with a view to offering recommendations to its parent bodies.

A. ASSESSMENT

Reviewing its work 1999-2005, the JWG recognizes that its performance has been stronger in some respects than others.

In response to the 1966 mandate "to stimulate the search for visible unity" (cf. appendix A of this report), there has been an emphasis on the discussion and the development of texts on issues of theological and pastoral concern and on learning from the experience of local churches.

It might be good for the next JWG to give more attention to the task of "initiating evaluating and sustaining forms of cooperation between the WCC and the RCC". It may also be fruitful to pay greater attention to "ad hoc initiatives". The JWG recognizes with satisfaction that new forms of collaboration have developed during the years of its mandate, and that there is now a stronger commitment for this kind of exchange.

The new JWG might also consider how it could more effectively fulfil the mandate of "being a challenge to the parent bodies by proposing new steps and programmes".

B. SUGGESTIONS

With the experience of these years, the JWG offers the following comments.

The importance of ecumenical spirituality needs to be reflected in the way the JWG operates. Its meetings might, for instance, begin with a day of recollection or retreat. Although during this period we have valued the opportunity to share one another's liturgies, we believe that the new JWG could further develop the possibilities for sharing the riches of our spiritual traditions.

There is need for a clear and comprehensive orientation for JWG members at the beginning of each new term. It would be essential if new members were well briefed on the mandate and the history of the JWG since 1965.

It is important that the parent bodies try to ensure that those appointed as members appreciate the importance of consistent attendance, not least to maintain regional balance.

The "reception" of the JWG's efforts needs to be enhanced. With and beyond the reporting required by the two parent bodies, initiatives are required to make the JWG's work accessible to the churches more widely, more speedily and in a more user-friendly form. One possibility is that study guides might be developed, for example, for use in connection with the documents on baptism and dialogue.

One of the JWG's functions is to "facilitate the exchange of information about the progress of the ecumenical movement, especially at the local level" (1975 guidelines). This has been very fruitfully achieved among the members themselves, but we believe that the task of making the fruits of this work known needs more attention.

The link between the JWG and NCCs and REOs could be developed. In addressing issues related to the proclamation of the gospel in the varied cultural context of today, these links could be particularly valuable.

The work of the JWG is, first and foremost, a journey of faith. Worship has been central to its life. There have been many contacts with local churches, ranging from a church-sponsored orphanage in Lebanon to a migrant community in Sweden to courageous efforts at peace-building in Northern Ireland. Through it all, relationships have deepened, and trust has grown.

2. Joint Working Group study documents

The JWG has produced three significant studies during this mandate, which are commended for use in a wide variety of contexts.

2.1. ECCLESIOLOGICAL AND ECUMENICAL IMPLICATIONS OF A COMMON BAPTISM (APPENDIX C)

The gradual development within the modern ecumenical movement of a common understanding of baptism is one of the basic factors that have enabled long separated Christians to speak today of sharing a real though imperfect communion. Both multi-lateral (e.g., BEM) and bilateral dialogues have contributed to theological convergence and/or agreement on baptism.

The purpose of the JWG study document on the ecclesiological and ecumenical implications of a common baptism is to assist the churches to recognize what has been accomplished, and to build on it. The document therefore reviews important aspects of the growing convergence on baptism, noting the still-remaining differences. The text illustrates the ecumenical impact of what has been achieved by showing examples of the way common perspectives on baptism have helped foster changed relationships, in some cases full communion, between churches long separated.

Both the ecclesiological and the ecumenical implications of the growing common understanding of baptism highlighted in the study are important if further steps towards visible unity are to be taken. Ecclesiological implications, noted at the end of each of the document's first five sections, refer to issues uncovered in that section which also must be considered in dialogue in order to work towards a common understanding of the church. Ecumenical implications listed together in section six refer to pastoral or practical steps that might be taken now within the churches in order to receive and to build on the growing common understanding of baptism.

The JWG hopes that this study document will be used by the churches in various educational settings in order to deepen the appreciation that, even though the goal of visible unity has not yet been achieved, through a common baptism separated Christians already share deep bonds of communion.

The study proceeded in the following way. Initial material for reflection was presented to the JWG executive in January 2000, which included a summary of implications of baptism gleaned from many responses to BEM (Msgr John Radano) and an overview of current Faith and Order work on baptism (Rev. Dr Alan Falconer). These two members were asked to coordinate the project. The JWG plenary in May 2000 developed five main areas which became the focus of discussion for the study. Drafting meetings took place in 2001 and 2002 (Geneva), February 2003 (Rome) and September 2003 (Geneva). Work in progress on the study was presented each year for discussion at annual JWG meetings. Participating in various drafting sessions were Dr Eugene Brand, Rev. Dr Thomas Best, Fr Gosbert Byamungu, the Rev. Dr Alan Falconer, Dr Mark Heim, Prof. Nicholas Lossky, Dr Thomas Pott, Msgr John Radano, Dr Teresa Rossi and Dr Liam Walsh. Dr Teresa Rossi did additional research on media presentations on baptism for the project, and Dr William Henn contributed suggestions for improving certain aspects of an advanced draft of the text. Bishop David Hamid reviewed the advanced text for editorial clarity and consistency. The study was adopted by the JWG plenary in Chania, in May 2004.

2.2. Nature and Purpose of Ecumenical Dialogue (Appendix D)

When the JWG between the RCC and the WCC was formed in 1965, it began its work by reflecting on the nature of ecumenical dialogue. The report, published in 1967, has served as a useful framework for ecumenical dialogues for some thirty years.

Since that time, relations between Christian communions and churches have grown and developed. The dialogues have helped to shatter stereotypes and dispel misunderstandings, and have led to changed relationships between churches on the way to visible unity. In this period of thirty years, there has developed a culture of dialogue.

However, there has also developed a renewed confessionalism. Difficulties in processes of reception have also led to division within confessional traditions participating in dialogues. Are issues of ethics and culture, which have not necessarily been the subject of dialogue, now becoming the sources of division within and between churches?

It was therefore felt appropriate that the JWG explore again the nature and practice of dialogue in the light of the experiences of thirty years, and of the new challenges and opportunities for dialogue at the beginning of the third millennium.

To initiate the process, two presentations were made on this topic at the beginning of this mandate of the JWG by then Bishop Walter Kasper and the Rev. Dr Konrad Raiser (published in *The Ecumenical Review*, 52, 3, 2000).

The document draws on: extensive discussions from meetings of the JWG plenary in Beirut (2000) and Dromantine (2001), both regions where community tension exists and where processes of dialogue have been developed; the papers of Cardinal Kasper and the Rev. Dr Raiser; the 1967 document; and subsequent published reflections from a number of theologians engaged in processes of dialogue.

The statement points to the development of the culture of dialogue, examines different approaches and notes the impact of the dialogues in creating new relationships between churches and communities. In the light of thirty years' experience of dialogues involving the Catholic Church, it explores anew the theological basis of dialogue, elicits a number of principles of dialogue, and develops some theses on the spirituality and practice of ecumenical dialogue. Attention is paid to the question of "reception", and reflection is given on the difficulties and positive experiences of such reception processes. The document concludes with some challenges posed to dialogue in the 21st century and underlines how the culture of dialogue is an essential expression of the nature of Christian living and is a key element of the common pilgrimage of churches as they seek to be faithful to the prayer that all may be one... so that the world may believe (John 17:21).

The study proceeded in the following way. After the presentations on dialogue by then Bishop Walter Kasper and the Rev. Dr Konrad Raiser, the first plenary developed a series of issues to be considered in a study document on dialogue. A small drafting group consisting of Eden Grace, Dr Susan Wood, Msgr Felix Machado, Msgr John Radano and Rev. Dr Alan Falconer met in Cartigny, Switzerland (February 2003), and produced an initial draft. After discussions in the plenary in Bari, the text was further developed through e-mail correspondence and at a one-day drafting session in September 2003 (the Rev. Dr Alan Falconer, Msgr John Radano, Rev. Dr Thomas Best). After further discussion at the JWG executive meeting in November 2004, Bishop David Hamid was asked to review the text for editorial consistency. The study document was adopted by the JWG plenary at Chania, Crete, in May 2004.

2.3. "INSPIRED BY THE SAME VISION": ROMAN CATHOLIC PARTICIPATION IN NATIONAL AND REGIONAL COUNCILS OF CHURCHES (APPENDIX E)

Because the JWG is responsible for overseeing and fostering relationships between the RCC and the WCC, it is fitting that this body present an overview of the nature, extent and quality of participation by the Catholic Church in councils of churches and regional ecumenical organizations around the world. This is not the first time the JWG has conducted such a review, but contexts continue to evolve. The number of Roman Catholic bodies participating in councils of churches continues to increase. And so, as the study document "Inspired by the Same Vision" states, "After more than forty years of experience, the JWG is asking some basic questions about Roman Catholic involvement in national and regional councils of churches and other ecumenical instruments. What works well? What is not working well? Why?" That is the purpose of this study.

The document recognizes that in many regions of the world councils of churches are a primary means whereby relationships among churches are nurtured and advanced. All involved will admit that the path is not always smooth. The study attempts to look forthrightly at problems and challenges that inhibit participation by the Catholic Church, in an effort to stimulate constructive reflection on ways *through* difficulties. To the degree that "all in each place" have representatives at the ecumenical table, the quest for full visible Christian unity is enhanced.

Specific recommendations are offered at the conclusion of the document, proposing that "representatives of NCCs, REOs and episcopal conferences in places where the Roman Catholic Church is not in membership... should consider the document 'Inspired by the Same Vision' and reflect on the experience others have gleaned regarding Catholic participation". Governing bodies of councils of churches and Catholic bishops conferences in every setting are urged to read and reflect on the document, and to do so together. In addition, the PCPCU and the WCC should sponsor a new international consultation to bring together representatives of NCCs, REOs and episcopal conferences, especially from places where the Roman Catholic Church is not in membership.

The text is divided into eight sections: a statement of purpose, definition and history of Roman Catholic participation, evolving attitudes towards membership, the value and benefits of membership, issues and concerns, questions to consider, concluding observations and recommendations.

The text concludes with the words, "We pray that the document will strengthen appreciation for, understanding of, and participation in councils of churches."

The study proceeded in the following way. A JWG sub-committee, co-chaired by the Rev. Thomas Michel, SJ, and the Rev. Dr Diane C. Kessler, worked steadily on this project beginning with the second meeting in Dromantine, Northern Ireland (2001). The other members were Rev. David Gill, Rev. Prof. Viorel Ionita, Sr Joan McGuire, OP, and Bishop Paul Nabil Sayah, with the assistance of Msgr John Mutiso-Mbinda and Ms Teny

Pirri-Simonian, respectively of the PCPCU and WCC staff. The drafting group customarily met for two days prior to sessions of the full JWG, held a drafting session in Rome in March 2003, and worked during the year sharing drafts via email. The topic was discussed in plenary sessions of the JWG in 2001-2003, and was considered by the JWG executive committee.

In August 2002, Rev. Dr Kessler presented the early stages of the draft at a meeting of the general secretaries of national councils of churches at Bossey in Celigny, Switzerland, and invited their participation in a study-and-response process. A number of councils requested copies of the draft for consideration, and several responded with recommendations. Councils that requested the draft and/or offered responses included those from Austria, Britain and Ireland, France, India, Norway, Slovak Republic, Sudan, Swaziland, Sweden, Switzerland and Tanzania. The Protestant Federation of France undertook the translation of the draft text into French. A gathering of state council of churches executives in the United States discussed the topic in one of their annual meetings and offered input into the study. The input provided by these and other bodies significantly enhanced the quality of the study. The study document was adopted by the JWG plenary at Chania, Crete, in May 2004.

3.   Issues studied by the JWG

3.1. THEOLOGICAL ANTHROPOLOGY

The proposed study on theological anthropology emerged from discussion at the JWG meeting in Antelias, Lebanon, in May 2000. This area of common interest has become increasingly urgent due to a range of issues affecting the understanding and protection of the human person posed, for example, by bio-ethics, human sexuality and violence.

During the period 2000-2004 a number of sessions were held to discuss those issues. Papers were presented at the Dromantine and Bari plenaries by Bishop Marc Ouellet, Prof. Nicholas Lossky, Archbishop Jozef Zycinski, Bishop Donal Murray and Dr Teresa Rossi. The topics explored were biblical anthropology, theological anthropology, the concept of imago Dei, particularly in the writings of Pope John Paul II.

A small group was formed to begin the process of drafting a study document, but due to change of staff personnel the group was not able to meet and the JWG executive recommended that discussion of the question should continue but that substantive work be taken up by the 2006-13 JWG, who could use the papers and reports submitted to the present JWG as a basis for their discussion.

3.2. INTERCHURCH MARRIAGES

The issue of interchurch marriages has been on the agenda of the JWG at different periods of its mandate. For instance, from 2 to 4 October 1989 in Geneva the JWG held a consultation on interchurch marriage to "assess the difficulties and opportunities of interchurch marriages".

During the current mandate of the JWG, discussion on this issue began at the first meeting plenary in Antelias, Lebanon, in 2000, and from the start the JWG took account of its previous work. It acknowledged that this is still an important and urgent matter before the churches and recognized that many look to the JWG to contribute to the churches' response to this pastoral concern. The following steps were proposed as a service that the JWG might offer to the RCC and to member churches of the WCC who are continuing to work on the questions and problems associated with interchurch marriages:

- to identify the available materials on interchurch marriages; (Association of Interchurch Families)
- to study these materials to assess which factors are specific to the life of the churches, and which are more likely based on cultural considerations; (Association of Interchurch Families)
- to identify initiatives that may be helpfully shared across the churches.

It is with considerable disappointment that, due to a sheer limit of time and staff resources, this JWG was not able to act upon the recommendations from its first plenary meeting.

The JWG is acutely aware that the *theological* issues involved in interchurch marriage are extremely complex. Beyond the pastoral concerns lie far-reaching ecclesiological implications for the churches as well as challenges to the varied understandings of the sacramentality of marriage. Despite the limitations of time and resources, the JWG was committed to listen sensitively to current reflection in the churches on this pastoral issue, the source of considerable hurt and pain for many Christians. It recognized the particular wisdom and experience that the Interchurch Families Association can offer in this area. Consequently, in Dromantine in 2001, four presentations were made to the plenary:

- ecumenical and ecclesiological implications of interchurch marriages, by Dr Ruth Reardon (Association Interchurch Families);
- proposed ways to move forward, by the Rev. Canon Martin Reardon (Association Interchurch Families);
- comments on the *Ecumenical Directory*, by Bishop Donal Murray;
- a summary of the 1996 agreement on interchurch marriages between Catholic and Orthodox patriarchs in the Middle East, by Archbishop Paul Sayah.

The third plenary in Stjärnholm in 2002 devoted a session to the issue of interchurch marriages. Three papers were presented reflecting three distinct Christian traditions: Bishop Marc Ouellet spoke of the "Sacrament of Matrimony according to the Catechism of the Catholic Church", Rev. Prof. Viorel Ionita presented an Orthodox perspective, and Rev. David Gill spoke from the point of view of a church of the Reformation. The ensuing discussion revealed that there may be possibilities of convergence on matters of grace and sacrament and the JWG recognized that the issue of interchurch marriage was not unrelated to the implications of the recognition of common baptism.

The difficult theological issues notwithstanding, the JWG continued to underline the need to remind the member churches of the WCC and the RCC of their *pastoral* responsibilities towards couples in interchurch marriages.

4. Areas of shared concern regarding social issues

4.1. SOCIAL THOUGHT AND ACTION

Even though social thought and action have been on the JWG agenda from the beginning, it has been difficult in the term of this mandate to find adequate ways to collaborate in this area. Among the reasons are the different nature of the partners, one a church, the other a council of churches, and their different approaches to dealing with social questions. The JWG study document "The Ecumenical Dialogue on Moral Issues: Potential Sources of Common Witness or of Division" remains a useful resource for confronting moral issues.

However, because of the locations in which it has met, the JWG has been able to explore issues of peace and reconciliation. At its first plenary in Antelias, in post-civil war Lebanon, meetings with representatives of local churches afforded opportunities to reflect not only on the character of ecumenical relations there, but also on experiences of dealing with violence, conflict, and the possibilities of reconciliation.

In the second plenary, in Dromantine, Northern Ireland, there were discussions of the conflicts that had taken place in Northern Ireland. Papers were presented by Dr David Stevens of the Irish Council of Churches, Rev. Dr Alan Falconer, and Bishop Anthony Farquhar, Catholic Auxiliary Bishop of Down and Connor. The recommendations of the working party on sectarianism were presented and the Irish School of Ecumenics' project on reconciliation was described. A visit to Belfast provided opportunities to come to a deeper understanding, not only of the conflicts, but also of the efforts at reconciliation that were taking place. The members saw, for example, the efforts of the Anglican and Roman Catholic cathedrals to build bridges between the two peoples in conflict.

4.2. DECADE TO OVERCOME VIOLENCE (2001-10) (DOV)

Cooperation on the DOV began with contacts around the topic of small arms followed by an invitation from the WCC to the Pontifical Council for Justice and Peace to have a staff member serve on the DOV reference committee. Another opportunity for joint work between the DOV staff at the WCC and the Pontifical Council on Justice and Peace arose within the framework of an international coalition for the UN Decade for a Culture of Peace and Nonviolence for the Children of the World, based in Paris, France. The coalition was founded in the summer of 2003 and both the DOV coordination office and the PCJP are observing members of the international committee.

The DOV coordination office has made efforts to publicize on the DOV website organizations, events, resources and stories from within the RCC, so as to make visible the fact that the DOV initiative reaches far beyond the formal WCC membership. Dioceses, local parishes and interchurch joint efforts are given visibility. In some countries national justice and peace commissions are part of the ecumenical DOV effort. For example, the DOV study guide *Why Violence? Why Not Peace?* was translated into French in Belgium by a group under Catholic leadership.

The third plenary in Stjärnholm was able to consider rich input from three events. These included the "Ten Points of Commitment to Peace" proclaimed at an ecumenical and inter-religious gathering of religious leaders in Assisi, 24 January 2002, at the invitation of Pope John Paul II; the Brussels Declaration of 20 December 2001 from the meeting organized by Ecumenical Patriarch Bartholomew; and the statement of an inter-faith meeting organized by the Archbishop of Canterbury in Alexandria, Egypt, in January 2002. The JWG executive at its meeting in March 2003 suggested that the JWG might consider publishing these three statements, with introductions, as a contribution to the DOV.

The same plenary heard a presentation, "Global Peace, Global Conflict, and Human Responsibility" by Prof. Peter Wallensteen of Uppsala university. Dr Teresa Rossi presented a 90-page printed report produced by a seminar which she conducted on the DOV at the St Thomas Aquinas Pontifical University in Rome during the 2003 spring semester, the first seminar in a long-term programme she has introduced on DOV. The report has also been presented at the PCPCU and sent to the WCC offices.

Concerning the war in Iraq, the WCC organized a prayer service for peace on the day the bombardment began. The WCC, with the assistance of Archbishop Diarmuid Martin, then the permanent representative of the Holy See to the UN bodies in Geneva, and former member of the JWG, invited representatives of religious communities in the city and the diplomatic corps in Geneva to take part in the service.

There is much room for increased cooperation with both the Vatican and Catholic constituencies within the framework of the DOV.

4.3. OTHER CONTACTS BETWEEN RCC/WCC

4.3.1. *Refugees and migration*

Cordial relations have developed between the Pontifical Council for Pastoral Care of Migrants and Itinerant Peoples and the WCC staff working on this same area. WCC representatives participated in the fifth world congress for the pastoral care of migrants and refugees, held in Rome, 17-22 November 2003. In 2001, His Eminence Cardinal Stephen Fumio Hamao and Rev. Fr Michael Blum (president and under-secretary of the Pontifical Council) visited WCC staff in Geneva to discuss ways of working together more collaboratively. The Rev. Fr Frans Thoolen of the Pontifical Council staff participated in meetings of United Nations High Commissioner for Refugees (UNHCR) governing bodies, often serving as the representative of the Holy See in these meetings. The possibility of strengthening collaboration in the area of programme is limited by staff capacity.

Cooperation between Roman Catholic organizations and the WCC has been particularly strong in the area of refugees and migration. Since the Harare assembly, cooperation between WCC and Caritas International, the International Catholic Migration Commission (ICMC) and the Jesuit Refugee Service (JRS) has continued. The ICMC and the JRS both have representatives in Geneva and WCC staff work closely with them on a number of advocacy initiatives, particularly related to the work of the UNHCR. This cooperation is often expressed through participation in NGO networks, particularly the International Council of Voluntary Agencies. In addition, there is mutual consultation, sharing of information from respective networks, and discussion of common priorities. The WCC and Caritas International are members of the 9-member steering committee for humanitarian response. Caritas and WCC networks share similar concerns and complement each other's awareness of the importance of working through local and national organizations. Caritas International also has close relations with Action by Churches Together (ACT) and is invited to participate in the annual meetings of the ACT emergency committee.

4.3.2. Diakonia and development

Archbishop Paul Josef Cordes, President of the Pontifical Council *Cor Unum* which undertakes charitable work, visited Geneva and the WCC in 2002. He had conversations with the Council leadership and staff working in areas of common interest with *Cor Unum*. Following this visit, the WCC director of the churches' commission on international affairs strengthened the relationship with the WCC by representing the WCC in the *Cor Unum* plenary assembly in 2003, where he was a keynote speaker.

5. Topical issues: the documents *Dominus Iesus* and *Ecclesia de Eucharistia*

During the period of the present mandate of the JWG, the WCC members of JWG held discussions with the Roman Catholic partners on two documents, namely, the instruction *Dominus Iesus* (published in 2000) and the 2003 encyclical on the eucharist, *Ecclesia de Eucharistia*. Both documents have important ecumenical implications and therefore needed to be discussed. For that reason, following their publication, the JWG played a valuable role as a forum where a frank discussion of the documents could take place. This process of dialogue was useful for clarifying some of the misunderstandings about the purpose of issuing such documents on the part of the RCC. The very fact that the RCC is open to listening to the reactions of the WCC representatives is in itself an important sign of its commitment to ecumenical dialogue.

At the JWG plenary of May 2001, some members of the JWG shared reactions received from WCC member churches on the document *Dominus Iesus*. The WCC made use of this spirit of dialogue and openness to continue the discussion of this document through a subsequent exchange of communication with the PCPCU.

V. Prospects for the Future (2006-2013)

Revisiting the mandate

As the JWG approaches the end of this working period, the members are deeply convinced that "there continues to be a need for a forum enabling the RCC and the WCC to evaluate together the development of the ecumenical movement". The JWG has amply proven that it is a necessary, vital instrument for the growth of ecumenical relations and the facilitating of a joint Christian response to the needs of the people of our time. But the members also see reasons for revisiting the mandate originally given in 1966 and modified in 1975, and for giving further attention to the composition and working style of the JWG.

The members agree that the JWG, as a consultative forum, is truly capable of inspiring, directing and sustaining dialogue between the RCC and the WCC regarding issues of concern to the ecumenical movement, and of facilitating collaboration between the various organs and programmes of the WCC and the RCC. But it is clear that we live in a changing world, marked by the destabilizing effect of globalization on peoples' lives and cultures, that the ecumenical horizon is undergoing rapid change, and that the churches, within themselves and in their service to the human family, face new and demanding challenges which call for ever greater commitment to the search for visible unity and common witness.

The members of the JWG have bonded well during the period of their engagement and common toil. They have reached a level of mutual understanding and trust that has allowed them to examine the issues before them with objectivity and critical discernment. They now set before the parent bodies areas of common concern which need further attention on the part of the next JWG. They have a sense that the JWG has the potential to achieve even greater results, and that consultations between the RCC and the WCC on the JWG's way forward should stress the original aim of the group as primarily that of "discovering and assessing promising new possibilities for ecumenical development", and in "proposing new steps and programmes" as a challenge to the parent bodies (cf. guidelines for the future of the JWG, *Breaking Barriers: Nairobi 1975*, David M. Paton ed., 1975, pp. 276-78).

Recommendations from the Joint Working Group to the RCC and the WCC

The following areas of common concern require particular attention, either because of their potential to strengthen relations between the churches and between Christians at all levels, or because they are perceived as continuing sources of pain or reasons of scandal between divided Christians.

1. Among the first, we point to a clear convergence between all the members of the JWG regarding the need to promote a return to the spiritual roots of ecumenism. Crucial at the beginning of the ecumenical movement was the spiritual ecumenism that inspired the Week of Prayer for Christian Unity, the commission on Mission and Evangelism, and the Faith and Order commission. At the November 2003 plenary assembly of the PCPCU, Cardinal Kasper stated:

"When we speak of ecumenical spirituality, we do not use this word – which is unfortunately overused – to mean a spirituality that is vague, weak, merely sentimental, irrational and subjective, that does not take into account the objective doctrine of the church, or even ignores it. On the contrary, we mean the teaching of scripture, of the living tradition of the church, and of the outcomes of ecumenical dialogues that have been personally and totally assimilated, are infused with life and in contact with life. Mere ecumenical activism is destined to exhaust itself; merely academic debate among experts, no matter how important it may be, eludes the 'normal' faithful and touches only the margin of their hearts and lives. We can only expand the ecumenical movement by deepening it."

At the general assembly of the All Africa Conference of Churches, Yaoundé, Cameroon, in November 2003, Rev. Dr Samuel Kobia, general secretary-designate of the World Council of Churches, said:

"From baptism to communal sharing of meals and reception of the spirit, the memory of Christ's suffering, death and resurrection becomes a reality in anticipation of another reality. The past in our minds is memory. Human beings cannot create, or even imagine, anything that is entirely new. But in the eucharistic meal something new always happens. Christ, in whose suffering our suffering as a community of faith is embodied, creates a new community. Once incorporated into the body one is expected to live by the mind of Christ in order to function fully and bring health to the life of the body. Activity within the body of Christ produces a new group identity and world-view. And by extension we can claim this ecclesiology as part of our ecumenism/ecumenical spirit...

"It is vitally important that we bring theology back to the people, and craft new themes of spirituality that are congenial to our unique experience and place in the world. We must re-emphasize the need for spirituality as the basis for the work we do in the world. That way we avoid being tantalized by the trappings of prestige that come with power even when such power is derived from a moral imperative...

"If we have the courage and tenacity of our forebears, who stood firmly like a rock against the lashes of slavery, we shall find a way to do in our times what they did for theirs and be awakened someday by the hope to a new dream come true."

What is needed is a renewed ecumenical spirituality based on the riches of our respective traditions, centred on continual conversion to Christ, able to intensify at the spiritual level relations between the ecumenical partners. We must be convinced that only by enriching one another spiritually, through common prayer and other forms of spiritual sharing, will it be possible for Christians successfully to tackle the important questions before us in dealing with one another and with the world around us. A return to the spiritual roots of ecumenism must be an aspect of any reflection on the renewal of the ecumenical movement itself.

2. We likewise agree that greater effort is needed in the field of ecumenical formation. Both parent bodies need to be concerned about Christians and clergy who need ecumenical formation. A new generation of Christians is sometimes unaware of the way things were and how much things have changed in the decades since the founding of the WCC and since the Second Vatican Council. In this respect much is being done, but we advocate an effort to improve the coordination of such formation through a more effective sharing of information and resources, and by providing greater opportunities for participation in each other's life. We especially recommend that the JWG keep before the churches the importance of offering young people opportunities to be exposed to traditions other than their own, especially in shared programmes of formation, mission and service. We also recommend the valuable study by the last JWG on ecumenical formation (cf. *Seventh Report of the JWG*, 1998, pp.57-59).

3. Among the areas of concern that are already having serious consequences for the churches and for ecumenical relations we point to the continuing, pressing, possibly church-dividing difficulties encountered in giving common witness in the field of personal and social moral issues. Society is becoming more confused and fragmented in its understanding of what it means to be truly human. Consequently, all churches are being called to respond to society's profound questioning in important matters of bio-ethics, human, civil and religious rights, issues of peace, social justice, healing of memories, human sexuality and reproduction. We believe that the JWG should, as a matter of urgency and in cooperation with Faith and Order and in consultation with other bodies, seek ways to develop the already-begun joint exploration of the philosophical and theological foundations of Christian anthropology. The 1991-98 JWG offered a valuable document in 1996: "The Ecumenical Dialogue on Moral Issues: Potential Sources of Common Witness or of Divisions". This 1998-2005 JWG has followed the topic closely (cf. *Seventh Report*, 1998, appendix B, p.31) and strongly recommends that it be carried forward into the next mandated period.

4. Other new challenges to Christians demand a response. Inter-religious dialogue has become an urgent necessity and Christians have to engage in this together. Religious pluralism and, in some places, the increasing absence of God in cultural life are challenging Christians to "give an account of the hope that is in [them]" (1 Pet. 3:15) and to live out together [their] common calling to mission. The spread of modern technology and the power of the media to form people's opinion and even their perception of reality calls for Christians to be responsibly critical towards the ensuing style of interpersonal, family and social relationships, and to be more effective in using the positive opportunities that these instruments offer. The prevalence of injustice, different forms of violence and the fear induced by international terrorism are directly opposed to the respect for human dignity that is at the heart of the Christian message. These are among the issues which can fruitfully be examined by the next JWG, as it seeks ways to improve and intensify cooperation between the churches.

We recommend therefore that in preparing the next JWG the parent bodies stress those parts of the original mandate that have perhaps been less to the forefront and which, nevertheless, are especially indicative of what is now needed. The JWG should be alert to identifying and proposing fresh forms of collaboration between the WCC and the RCC. The members should be asked to commit more effort to interpreting the major streams of ecumenical thought at the general and local levels, without undertaking study processes which are or could be carried out by other bodies.

In response to the changing needs of the ecumenical task, the JWG might fruitfully reflect on how its work can be related more closely to the context and praxis in different local situations around the world. Like flexibility and adaptability to the changing circumstances of the mission entrusted by Christ to his disciples (cf. Matt. 28:19) these are also essential qualities of the ecumenical cooperation which are also required of the JWG itself.

The task of the JWG is in fact to facilitate the advent of a time when the RCC and the WCC member churches can meet in genuine *koinonia* and can therefore give convincing witness to the world of the transforming message of the gospel of Jesus Christ. We entrust the work of the past seven years to the Triune God and pray that the Holy Spirit "will bring to completion the work he has begun in us" (cf. Phil. 1:6).

Members of the Joint Working Group
1999-2006

**Representatives of the
Roman Catholic Church**

Most Rev. Mario CONTI
Co-Moderator JWG
Archbishop of Glasgow
Glasgow, UK

Most Rev. Walter KASPER
1999-2001
Secretary
Pontifical Council
for Promoting Christian Unity
Vatican City

Most Rev. Marc OUELLET
2001-2003
Secretary
Pontifical Council
for Promoting Christian Unity
Vatican City

Most Rev. Brian FARRELL
since 2003
Secretary
Pontifical Council
for Promoting Christian Unity
Vatican City

Most Rev. Giampaolo CREPALDI
since 2001
Pontifical Council for
Justice and Peace
Vatican City

Most Rev. Michael FITZGERALD
1999-2002
Pontifical Council
for Interreligious Dialogue
Vatican City

Most Rev. Diarmuid MARTIN
1999-2001
Pontifical Council
for Justice and Peace
Vatican City

Most Rev. Donal B. MURRAY
Bishop of Limerick
Limerick, Ireland

Most Rev. Donald J. REECE
Bishop of St John's Basseterre
St John's, Antigua, West Indies

Most Rev. Paul Nabil SAYAH
Archbishop of Haifa
and the Holy Land (Maronite)
Jerusalem

Most Rev. Buti J. TLHAGALE, OMI
Archbishop of the Diocese
of Johannesburg
Doornfontein, South Africa

Most Rev. Józef M. ZYCINSKI
Archbishop of Lublin
Lublin, Poland

Rev. Dr Remi HOECKMAN
1999-2001
Pontifical Council for
Promoting Christian Unity
Vatican City

Rev. Monsignor
Felix A. MACHADO
since 2002
Pontifical Council for
Interreligious Dialogue
Vatican City

Sister ?John McGUIRE, OP
Ecumenical Officer
Archdiocese of Chicago
Chicago IL, USA

Sister Celine MONTEIRO, FMM
Franciscan Missionaries of Mary
Generalate, Rome
Rome, Italy

Sister Elizabeth MORAN, MSSC
World Council of Churches
Mission and Ecumenical Formation
Geneva, Switzerland

Rev. Monsignor
John MUTISO-MBINDA
Co-Secretary JWG
Pontifical Council
for Promoting Christian Unity
Vatican City

Rev. Monsignor
John A. RADANO
Pontifical Council
for Promoting Christian Unity
Vatican City

Dr Teresa Francesca ROSSI
Centro Pro Unione
Roma, Italy

Sister Theresa SEOW, FdCC
St Anthony's Canossian Convent
Singapore

Ms Denise SULLIVAN
1999-2000 (passed away)
Catholic Bishop's Committee
for Ecumenical and Interfaith Relations
Mawson ACT 2607, Australia

Rev. Father
Juan USMA GÓMEZ
Since 2001
Pontifical Council
for Promoting Christian Unity
Vatican City

Rev. Father
Thomas MICHEL, SJ
Consultant since 2001
Secretary for Interreligious Dialogue
Jesuit Curia
Rome, Italy

Administrative staff

Dr Paola FABRIZI
Pontifical Council for
Promoting Christian Unity
Vatican City

**Representatives
of the World Council of Churches**

Bishop Dr Jonas JONSON
Church of Sweden (Lutheran)
Co-Moderator JWG
Bishop of Strängnäs
Strängnäs, Sweden

Prof. Dr Oscar CORVÁLAN-
VÁSQUEZ
Pentecostal Church of Chile
Talca, Chile

Rt Rev. Bishop H. Mvume DANDALA
Methodist Church of South Africa
General Secretary
All Africa Conference of Churches
Nairobi, Kenya

His Grace Metropolitan
Philipos Mar EUSEBIUS
Malankara Orthodox Syrian Church
St Basil Aramana
Kerala, India

His Eminence Metropolitan Prof. Dr
GENNADIOS OF SASSIMA
Ecumenical Patriarchate
of Constantinople
Istanbul, Turkey

Rev. David GILL
Uniting Church in Australia
Kowloon
Hong Kong SAR, China

Rt Rev. David HAMID
Anglican Consultative Council
Suffragan Bishop in Europe
Westminster, London, UK

Rev. Prof. Viorel IONITA
Romanian Orthodox Church
Study Secretary
Conference of European Churches
Geneva, Switzerland

Dr Musimbi KANYORO
Lutheran
General Secretary
World Young Women's
Christian Association
Geneva, Switzerland

Ms Ülle KEEL
Estonian Evangelical Lutheran Church
Tallinn, Estonia

Rev. Dr Diane C. KESSLER
United Church of Christ, USA
Executive Director
Massachusetts Council of Churches
Boston, USA

Prof. Nicholas LOSSKY
Russian Orthodox Church
Paris, France

Rev. Valamotu PALU
Free Wesleyan Church of Tonga
General Secretary
Pacific Conference of Churches
Suva, Fiji

Rev. Dr Alan FALCONER
Director, Faith and Order
World Council of Churches
Geneva, Switzerland

Mr Georges LEMOPOULOS
Deputy General Secretary
World Council of Churches
Geneva, Switzerland

Ms Teny PIRRI-SIMONIAN
Co-Secretary JWG
Church and Ecumenical Relations
World Council of Churches
Geneva, Switzerland

Administrative staff

Ms Luzia WEHRLE
Administrative Assistant
Church and Ecumenical Relations
World Council of Churches
Geneva, Switzerland

JWG Mandates: 1966, 1975 and 1999-2005

I. Mandate 1966 (from the seventh report of the Joint Working Group between the Roman Catholic Church and the World Council of Churches, Geneva-Rome, 1998, p.3):

The JWG functions according to its original 1966 mandate as modified by the 1975 WCC assembly.

1. The JWG is a consultative forum. It has no authority in itself but reports to its parent bodies – the WCC assembly and central committee, and the PCPCU – which approve policies and programmes.

   It undertakes its spiritual and pastoral tasks in a spirit of prayerful conviction that God through Christ in the Spirit is guiding the one ecumenical movement. The group tries to discern the will of God in contemporary situations, and to stimulate the search for visible unity and common witness, in particular through collaboration at world, regional, national and local levels between the RCC, the WCC, and the WCC member churches. This means giving attentive support and encouragement to whatever contributes to ecumenical progress.

   The JWG initiates, evaluates and sustains forms of collaboration between the WCC and the RCC, especially between the various organs and programmes of the WCC and the RCC. Its styles and forms of collaboration are flexible, as it discerns similarities and differences which foster or hinder WCC/RCC relations. Concentrating on ad hoc initiatives, it keeps new structures to a minimum in proposing new steps and programmes, carefully setting priorities and using its limited resources of personnel, time and finances.

2. At present the JWG has 17 members, with two co-moderators. Its co-secretaries are a PCPCU staff member and the WCC's deputy general secretary responsible for relations with non-member churches. Most members are involved in pastoral and ecumenical ministries in different regions. Some are from departments of the Roman Curia and from the WCC units. The JWG also co-opts consultants for its particular tasks. The co-moderators, co-secretaries and four others form the executive, which oversees the JWG between its plenaries and prepares the agenda and materials for them.

II. Mandate 1975 (from *Breaking Barriers: Nairobi 1975*, David M. Paton ed., 1975, pp.276-78)

CONTINUATION OF THE JOINT WORKING GROUP

There continues to be the need for a forum enabling the Roman Catholic Church and the World Council of Churches to evaluate together the development of the ecumenical movement. Therefore a joint group with continuity of membership and sufficient breadth of representation from both sides should be appointed. As an instrument of the parent bodies it will be in close contact with them and accountable to them.

THE FUNCTIONS OF THE JOINT WORKING GROUP

The Joint Working Group will primarily aim at discovering and assessing promising new possibilities for ecumenical development. It has the task of stimulating discussion on the ecumenical movement, seeking to be a challenge to the parent bodies by proposing new steps and programmes.

The Joint Working Group will endeavour to interpret the major streams of ecumenical thought and action in the Roman Catholic Church and in the member churches of the World Council of Churches. It will facilitate the exchange of information about the progress of the ecumenical movement, especially at the local level.

The Joint Working Group will seek to establish the collaboration between the various organs and programmes of the Roman Catholic Church and the World Council of Churches. In accordance with the principles and procedures of the parent bodies it should encourage the genuine development of any ecumenical collaboration. It should draw upon the insights gained from local experience to foster such collaboration. As in the past, it will remain a consultative group, not an operative agency. It may be empowered by the parent bodies to develop and administer programmes it has proposed when this is called for.

As the Joint Working Group seeks to initiate and help keep alive the discussion on the implications of the ecumenical movement in the Roman Catholic Church and in member churches of the World Council of Churches, it will seek the best means of communicating its findings and recommendations.

An essential aspect of its task is to share its findings with parent bodies.

EXPANDED RELATIONSHIP

The Joint Working Group will be in contact with a large number and range of ecumenical organizations and programmes, especially on the local level. It may call upon various offices and programmes of the parent bodies for assistance when special help is needed in certain areas in the process of collaboration. It will also seek information and advice from individuals and organizations which have particular ecumenical experience and competence.

FLEXIBLE STYLE

As the Joint Working Group seeks to meet the needs of the churches, the style of collaboration must be kept flexible. It must be adaptable to various and changing needs.

Therefore it will seek to keep new structures to a minimum while concentrating on ad hoc initiatives as they are required by the actual developments within the ecumenical movement. On occasion, of course, particular projects may call for some structural organization which will be set up after due authorization. Flexibility of style does not mean unplanned activity or lack of accountability. It rather means more careful attention to the setting of priorities and to the use of resources.

SUGGESTED STRUCTURES

On the basis of these general considerations the following is proposed:

1. The Joint Working Group shall be a group of approximately 16 members, some of whom shall be chosen from the staff of the World Council of Churches and the Secretariat for Promoting Christian Unity (and other organs of the Curia).

2. The Joint Working Group will normally meet once a year. Further, enlarged meetings could be held on occasion to deal with specific issues. Such meeting may be arranged to coincide with some important regional event when this is judged useful.

3. A small executive group of six members shall be responsible for the ongoing work between meetings and for preparing the meetings of the Joint Working Group.

III. Mandate 1999-2005 (from seventh report of the Joint Working Group between the Roman Catholic Church and the World Council of Churches, Geneva-Rome, 1998, p. 23):

The JWG recommends these specific priorities for the next period of its mandate:

ISSUE AFFECTING *KOINONIA*

The ecclesial consequences of common baptism. The implications of recognizing the common baptism of Christians on ecclesial communion and liturgical practice.

The ecumenical role of interchurch marriages. The ecclesiological implications of the sacrament of marriage between Christians of different churches and in their family life.

Local, national and regional councils of churches which have RC churches as full members. The practical and ecclesiological implications of membership of councils of churches, and their instrumental role in the growth of koinonia.

Church and church law. The impact of ecumenical agreements and dialogues on actual church legislation and on relations between eccesiology and canon law/church law/church discipline.

COMMON CONCERNS FACING THE WCC AND RCC

The stances of conservative Evangelicals and Charismatic/Pentecostals towards the ecumenical movement and its present structures. The establishing of dialogue.

Christian fundamentalists: an ecumenical challenge? The impact of fundamentalism on the ecumenical commitment of churches and on the agenda of dialogue.

The place of women in the churches. The further recognition and integration of the gifts of women in church life and society, and the appropriation of the findings of the Ecumenical Decade of the Churches in Solidarity with Women on the life, structures and witness of the churches.

Ecumenical education. The development of appropriate ecumenical education for church members, students and clergy on the fundamentals of the Christian life in the search for the manifestation of the unity of the church within a pluralist society.

APPENDIX B

The History of the RCC/WCC Joint Working Group

From the seventh report of the Joint Working Group between the Roman Catholic Church and the World Council of Churches, Geneva-Rome, 1998, pp.24-30: "The JWG expresses its gratitude for this short history, written on its request by one of its members, Father Thomas Stransky CSP, rector of the Tantur Ecumenical Institute, Jerusalem, 1998":

The initial visible expression of collaboration between the Roman Catholic Church (RCC) and the World Council of Churches (WCC) was the exchange of officially delegated observers. In 1961 the Vatican Secretariat for Promoting Christian Unity (SPCU), which Pope John XXIII had established in June 1960, delegated five observers to the WCC's third assembly in New Delhi. Then the WCC sent two observers, Dr Nikos Nissiotis and Dr Lukas Vischer, to the four autumn sessions of the Second Vatican Council (1962-65).

During the Vatican II years, the SPCU arranged for the RC New Testament scholar Fr Raymond Brown to give a major address on the unity of the church to the 1963 world conference of Faith and Order in Montreal. That same year, two SPCU observers, Frs Jorge Mejia and Thomas Stransky, participated in the first world conference of the WCC's division of World Mission and Evangelism (DWME) in Mexico City. In 1965 the SPCU co-sponsored meetings with DWME and the WCC Church and Society department to discuss the Vatican II drafts on the missionary activity of the church and on the church in the modern world.

In November 1964, the 2200 bishops and Pope Paul VI promulgated the Vatican II Decree on Ecumenism, which was the official charter of the RCC's active participation in the one ecumenical movement, described as being "fostered by the grace of the Holy Spirit" for "the restoration of unity among all Christians" who "invoke the Triune God and confess Jesus as Lord and Saviour" – an allusion to the WCC basis.

Anticipating this Decree, SPCU and WCC representatives began in April 1964 to consider future RCC-WCC collaboration. They proposed a joint working group with a five-year experimental mandate. In January 1965 the WCC central committee, meeting in Enugu, Nigeria, adopted the proposal, as did the RCC authorities in February, through SPCU president Cardinal Augustin Bea, during his visit to the WCC in Geneva.

The main points of the original mandate of the JWG still function:

1. The JWG has no authority in itself, but is a consultative forum. It initiates, evaluates and sustains collaboration between the WCC and the RCC, and reports to the competent authorities: the WCC assembly and central committee, and the Pontifical Council (prior to 1988 the Secretariat) for Promoting Christian Unity (PCPCU). The parent bodies may empower the JWG to develop and administer programmes it has proposed.

2. The JWG seeks to be flexible in the styles of collaboration. It keeps new structures to a minimum, while concentrating on ad hoc initiatives in proposing new steps and programmes, and carefully setting priorities and using its limited resources in personnel and finances.

3. The JWG does not limit its work to the administrative aspects of collaboration. It tries also to discern the will of God in the contemporary ecumenical situation, and to offer its own reflections in studies.

With eight WCC and six RCC members, the JWG had its first meeting in May 1965, at the Ecumenical Institute at Bossey, near Geneva. The two co-chairpersons were the WCC general secretary, Dr W.A. Visser 't Hooft, and the SPCU secretary Bishop Johannes Willebrands. By late 1967 the JWG had published its first two official reports (February 1966 and August 1967).

These reports offered a wide-ranging agenda for RCC-WCC collaboration in study and activities which could serve the one ecumenical movement: the nature of ecumenism and methods of ecumenical dialogue; common prayer at ecumenical gatherings; joint preparation of materials for the annual Week of Prayer for Christian Unity; a common date for Easter; the RCC's direct bilateral dialogues with other churches; collaboration in missionary activities in the context of religious freedom, witness and proselytism; the place of the church in society; Christian responsibility in international affairs, especially in the promotion of peace and justice among peoples and nations; collaboration in social service, in emergency and development aid and in medical work; cooperation of men and women in church, family and society; laity and clergy training; mixed marriages between Christians.

At the WCC fourth assembly (Uppsala 1968), two Catholics addressed plenary sessions. The Jesuit Roberto Tucci put the agenda of the JWG in the light of the RCC's self-understanding in the modern world, as expressed in the 16 documents of Vatican II, and in view of developments in the WCC and its member churches since the first assembly in Amsterdam in 1948. And Lady Ward Jackson pressed for the common witness of all the churches in response to the crises in world hunger and development, justice and peace.

The Uppsala assembly and the SPCU ratified the work of the JWG and its proposals for future RCC-WCC collaboration, and approved the admission of 12 RCs as full members of the Faith and Order commission.

The Uppsala assembly already occasioned the question of the eventual membership of the RCC as such in the WCC.

A year after the Uppsala assembly, the WCC general secretary, Dr Eugene Carson Blake, invited Pope Paul VI to visit the WCC headquarters in Geneva. On 10 June 1969 the pope did so. In the chapel before a common prayer service, he expressed "without hesitation" his "profound appreciation" for the work of the JWG in the development of the "relations between the World Council and the Catholic Church, two bodies indeed different in nature, but whose collaboration has proved to be faithful". The pope judged the question of RCC membership in the WCC to be "still an hypothesis. It contains serious theological and pastoral implications. It thus requires profound study."

During its second five-year mandate, the JWG began to study the membership question. It became aware that, despite a shared commitment to common witness within the one ecumenical movement, the disparity between the two parent bodies affects the extent, style and content of collaboration.

The WCC is a fellowship of independent churches, most of them nationally organized; and its members do not take direct juridical responsibility for WCC studies, actions and statements. The RCC is one church with a universal mission and structure of teaching and governance as an essential element of its identity. The RCC understands itself as a family of local churches with and under the bishop of Rome, and its structures of decision-making on the world and national (through the bishops conferences) levels differ from those of the WCC's member churches. Furthermore, representation of member churches on WCC governing bodies must give "due regard" to size. Given that there are almost twice as many RC members as adherents of all the WCC member churches combined, the consequences for achieving such balanced representation were the RCC to become a member would be enormous unless the WCC structures would radically change.

Although not insuperable obstacles, these were the main reasons why the RCC, in evaluating the JWG study of the advantages and disadvantages of membership, decided in 1972 not to ask for WCC membership "in the immediate future". But in that reserved response was the conviction that through the JWG "collaboration between the RCC and the WCC must not only continue, but be intensified". The JWG's time and energy shifted from the membership issue to improved collaboration.

As the JWG's third report (1970) stipulated, the cooperation within the JWG is "only a limited section of the whole field of ecumenical collaboration, and one which cannot be isolated from the ecumenical movement as a whole". Since Vatican II, an array of collaborative activities between Catholics and WCC member churches had appeared on parish, local and national levels; and full RC membership in national and regional councils or conferences of churches was beginning to take place. This would be documented in the 1975 survey published by the SPCU, *Ecumenical Collaboration at the Regional, National and Local Levels*.

While the presence of RC members on the Faith and Order commission meant that the JWG could now leave certain important theological and liturgical questions to that commission, it did continue its own studies; for example, *Common Witness, Religious Freedom and Proselytism* (1970). WCC staff contacts with the Vatican Congregation for the Evangelization of Peoples led to the appointment of consultants from SEDOS, a working partnership of Catholic missionary orders of men and of women, to the WCC division of World Mission and Evangelism.

The theme of the October 1974 RC bishops synod was "evangelization in the modern world". A year earlier the preparatory draft for the synod had been sent not only to the episcopal conferences but also to the WCC for comments and suggestions. The synod invited the WCC general secretary, Dr Philip Potter, to address one of its plenary sessions. He noted that the major problems and challenges of evangelization on the synod's agenda were the same as those on the agenda of the WCC: "Evangelization is essentially an ecumenical enterprise."

Experts, appointed by the Vatican Secretariat for Non-Believers (since 1983, the Pontifical Council for Interreligious Dialogue), joined in WCC consultations with Buddhist, Christian, Hindu and Muslim scholars (Lebanon 1970), and with other Christians on the theological implications of the dialogue between people of living faiths (Zurich 1970).

The JWG facilitated forms of RCC-WCC collaboration with the Christian Medical Commission (WCC), the Laity Council (RCC) and international women's groups.

In 1968 the WCC and the new Pontifical Commission for Justice and Peace (1967) sponsored a large interdisciplinary conference on development (Beirut). It brought together theologians and church leaders from "developed and developing" countries, representatives from international secular organizations and leading experts in world politics and economics. The successful conference gave impetus to the JWG proposal for a joint committee on society, development and peace (SODEPAX). Headquartered in Geneva, with generous independent funding, SODEPAX quickly responded to the widespread local and national initiatives by helping them to set up their own SODEPAX groups, and by offering them the results of its own practical and theological studies on social communication, education for development, mobilization for peace and working with peoples of other world faiths.

The JWG also facilitated the initial consultations between RC relief organizations and the WCC division of Interchurch Aid, Refugees and World Service. These quickly led to steady and normal ways of exchanging information, reciprocal consultation, and to joint planning and coordination of material relief, especially in cases of sudden physical disasters and wars that result in massive movements of refugees.

In 1975, prior to the WCC's fifth assembly (Nairobi), the JWG's fourth report looked back on RCC-WCC dialogue and collaboration during the ten years since the promulgation of the Decree on Ecumenism: "Where have we been led during these ten years? What has been achieved? What should and can be our goal in the years to come? How should the RCC and the WCC relate to one another, in order to serve and further the ecumenical movement?"

The fourth report offered three perspectives on "the common ground" for relations between the RCC, the member churches and the WCC itself:

1. The Triune God "gathers together the people of the New Covenant as a *communion* of unity in faith, hope and love". This communion continues to exist, but because of Christian divisions, it is a "real but imperfect" communion. The ecumenical movement – "the restoration of the unity of all Christians" – is "the common rediscovery of that existing reality and equally the common efforts to overcome the obstacles standing in the way of perfect ecclesial communion". This vision of "real and full communion" is "far from being fulfilled, and even its concrete shape cannot yet be fully described, but it has already become part of the life of the churches". In fact, "work for the unity of the church is… an inescapable reality. It is not a luxury which can be left aside, nor a task which can be handed to specialists but rather a constitutive dimension of the life of the church at all levels and of the life of Christians themselves".

2. The gift of communion calls for the response of *common witness* to Christ in the world, "wherever the partial communion in faith and life, as it exists among the

churches, makes it possible... Mission without unity lacks the perspective of the body of Christ, and unity without mission is not a living reality."

3.   This real but imperfect communion in today's world calls for a shared commitment to the *renewal of Christians and of the churches*, as they together engage "to discern and interpret the signs of the times" and "to struggle for justice, freedom and community" and for a more human society.

This "common ground" shapes the vision of the JWG and continues to orient its activities. On the one hand, the JWG realizes it is only one structure in the manifold and diverse – official and unofficial – ecumenical movement at every level of the churches' life. On the other hand, as a joint instrument the JWG is more specifically influenced by developments and changes within its parent bodies.

Collaboration with the WCC Ecumenical Institute at Bossey has continued. A Roman Catholic professor was appointed to the faculty, and each year its graduate school students and staff journey to Rome for meetings with various departments of the Roman Curia, with professors at the universities, with members of the Unions of Superiors General (male and female religious communities) and with leaders of international and local lay movements. In 1984 a Roman Catholic sister became a full-time consultant to the Geneva staff of the commission on World Mission and Evangelism.

But a withdrawal of structural collaboration occurred with SODEPAX. Caught in the dilemma of being regarded as a "third entity" by the WCC offices in Geneva and the Vatican authorities or of becoming an over-structured instrument for liaison between separate activities of its parent bodies, SODEPAX reduced its operations, and in 1980 its experimental mandate was finally terminated. In fact, the JWG has yet to find the proper structured ways of collaboration in social thought and action.

In June 1984, Pope John Paul II visited the WCC in Geneva. The pope asked the JWG to be "imaginative in finding the ways which here and now allow us to join in the great mission of revealing Christ to the world. In doing his truth together we shall manifest his light." Besides the formal addresses and the common prayer service, John Paul II and WCC senior staff had an open-ended, off-the-record discussion on ecclesiological issues and social-political challenges.

In April 1986, the WCC general secretary, Dr Emilio Castro, led a delegation to Rome, where they met not only with the pope but with senior Vatican staff and others.

The JWG's fifth report, prepared for the sixth WCC assembly (Vancouver 1983), reflected on the changes transforming the cultural, social and political relations between nations and peoples. "The human family becomes more aware that it faces either a common future or a common fate", and more people everywhere are becoming "conscious of their solidarity and of standing together in defence of justice and human dignity, their own and that of others". For many, "religion, with its claim to be a source of hope, is questioned and labelled as a way of easy escape from the world's predicament". For others, "the gospel is shared by human hearts, hands are joined in confident prayer". These Christians experience that "more than ever before, the divisions among Christians appear as a scandal", and that Christians are being drawn together as "agents of reconciliation".

The fifth report noted "a new 'tradition' of ecumenical understanding, shared concerns and common witness at all levels of the churches' life". During the almost twenty years since Vatican II, renewed awareness in the RCC of the inter-relation of the local church in bonds of communion with the other local churches and with the See of Rome "has opened up new possibilities for understanding the place of unity and diversity within the church and the nature of ecclesial communion. But the practical implications of this and of the collegiality it implies are still being worked out in new initiatives and new pastoral structures such as episcopal conferences and other regional and local bodies, and it is these which have the primary responsibility for overseeing ecumenical activities."

In communicating the RC authorities' approval of the fifth report to the WCC general secretary, Dr Philip Potter, the SPCU president Cardinal Willebrands suggested that rather than designating the relationship of the RCC to the WCC as "collaboration", one might use Pope Paul VI's term "fraternal solidarity". This is a better description, for it connotes "not only collaboration but also common reflection and prayer, inspired by the words of Christ 'that all may be one'", and it expresses "our common calling to full communion in faith and love".

The Vancouver response to the fifth report says that the experiences which are drawing the churches together reveal that "diversity in witness which responds to different pastoral situations and contemporary challenges" is not "a sign of dividedness in faith but of enrichment of the common faith of the church". The response continues: "The churches assign different degrees of significance to formulated doctrine and authoritative teaching as criteria for unity within and among the churches. The experiences of common witness can help them to discover afresh the source of their faith beyond the differences of inherited doctrinal formulations." But two major questions remain on the ecumenical agenda: How much diversity in doctrine, moral teaching and witness is compatible with the confession of the one apostolic faith in the one church? And behind this: What is the authority of and in the church?

The sixth report, in preparation for the WCC's seventh assembly (Canberra 1991), refers to the RCC's lengthy response (1987) to the 1982 Lima document on *Baptism, Eucharist and Ministry* (BEM) – the first time the RCC had given an official response to an ecumenical document from the WCC. Critically important was the broad discussion process which led to the RC response, which introduced the WCC, in particular its Faith and Order commission, to a wide variety of RC bodies which submitted their own BEM study reports to the PCPCU for synthesis and analysis: bishops conferences, theological faculties and other bodies. In addition, BEM was discussed on national and local levels by ecumenical groups, seminars, commissions, seminaries, university faculties of theology, ecumenical institutes, popular magazines and journals.

By 1990 the RCC was a full member of over 35 NCCs and of regional ecumenical organizations in the Caribbean, Middle East and Pacific; and it had close working relationships with other national and regional councils or conferences. A world consultation of these councils of churches in Geneva in 1986 discussed the implications of these direct forms of RC participation, in the context of their ecclesiological significance in the ecumenical movement, and specific varied aspects of mission and dialogue, finance and resource-sharing, and social and political challenges. This development increased in the 1990s, helping to decentralize the work of the JWG and allowing the group to focus more of its attention on international issues and new challenges on the horizon.

On the theological level, the JWG commissioned a study on *The Church: Local and Universal*. Published in 1990, it dealt with the mystery of the church in its local and universal expressions, with the interpretation of "ecclesial communion" by the RCC, the WCC assemblies and the various Christian communions, and with how these communions use canonical structures to express and safeguard communion within their churches. Another JWG study document was *The Hierarchy of Truths* (1990). The nature of faith is organic. Revealed truths organize around and point to the centre or foundation – the person and mystery of Jesus Christ. By better understanding the ways in which other Christians hold, express and live the faith, each confessional tradition can also be led to a better understanding of itself and see its own formulations of doctrine in a broader ecumenical perspective – the foundational content of what, in common witness, should be proclaimed in word and life in a way that speaks to the religious needs of the human spirit. This study thus complements the 1980 JWG study on *Common Witness and Proselytism* (1980).

The JWG also noted the proliferation of joint Bible translation, publication and distribution; common Bible studies; collaboration in the press, television and other means of communication; use of the Ecumenical Prayer Cycle; the Week of Prayer for Christian Unity and other expressions of common prayer.

The RCC appointed twenty experts as advisers to the 1990 world convocation on justice, peace and the integrity of creation (Seoul, Korea); in addition, a number of RCs were full participants in the convocation as members of delegations of NCCs or regional ecumenical bodies of which the RCC is a member. Participation of this type is now customary in WCC assemblies and other world meetings and consultations. WCC- and RC-related organizations co-sponsored a meeting in Brussels in 1988 on the European Community and the debt crisis of African, Caribbean and Pacific countries.

This short history of the JWG, which can only suggest a few highlights of RCC-WCC collaboration and "fraternal solidarity", continues in the seventh report, 1991-98. By comparing the seven JWG reports from 1966 to 1997, one sees that by the time of the sixth and seventh reports nearly all programmatic activities of the WCC have RC representation. But as WCC general secretary Konrad Raiser observed in 1995, "What remains an open question is how all these experiences are shared at the local level and serve local ecumenical cooperation. The JWG has not yet found an effective way to respond to this aspect of the task."

Ecclesiological and Ecumenical Implications of a Common Baptism

A JWG Study

Introduction

1. In baptism one is brought into the saving mysteries of the reconciliation of humanity with God through Jesus Christ. Baptism creates a unique relationship to Christ because it is a participation in his life, death and resurrection. (cf. *Baptism, Eucharist and Ministry* (BEM), 1982, B3).

2. "Through Baptism, Christians are brought into union with Christ, with each other and with the church of every time and place" (B6), the community which is formed by the healing grace of Christ. Many persons experience the sorrows and anguish of broken social relations and broken family life, with all the devastating impact that brokenness can have on those concerned. The world itself shows signs of fractured human relationships: structures of alienation and division contradict that unity which God intends for all peoples and creation (Col. 1:15). But baptism is the joyful act of welcome into a new and caring community of the faithful bound together in Jesus Christ – a community which transcends the very divisions evident in society. Life in Christ brought about by baptism is a healing balm for individuals and community alike, in a broken and sinful world.

3. While divided churches themselves contradict God's reconciliation in Christ, one of the great achievements of the modern ecumenical movement has been to show that, as Pope John Paul II has stated, "the universal brotherhood of Christians has become a firm ecumenical conviction... [and this]... is rooted in recognition of the oneness of baptism..." (*Ut Unum Sint* 42). It is because of baptism and our allegiance to Christ that we can call one another Christians. Indeed on the basis of a common recognition of baptism into Christ, some churches have been enabled to enter new relationships of communion. Such recognition is not simply a statement of how an individual's baptism is regarded, "it constitutes an ecclesiological statement" (*ibid.*). Individual members of churches should not be considered apart from the whole community of faith that gave them birth and in which they are nourished and exercise Christian discipleship. This study therefore seeks to explore the ecclesiological and ecumenical implications of a common recognition of baptism.

4. In undertaking the study the Joint Working Group has drawn on the insights of international bilateral and multilateral discussions on baptism and on official responses to BEM. It has also taken into account a survey of agreements on the recognition of baptism undertaken by the Pontifical Council for Promoting Christian Unity and continuing work on baptism being conducted by the Faith and Order commission of the WCC.

BAPTISM IN THE MODERN ECUMENICAL MOVEMENT

5. In the modern ecumenical movement, the gradual acknowledgment of a common understanding of baptism has been one of the most basic reasons enabling long separated Christians to speak now of sharing a real though incomplete communion. According to the Faith and Order convergence text *Baptism, Eucharist and Ministry*, which has gained wide acceptance among Christians of various traditions, "Through baptism, Christians are brought into union with Christ, with each other, and with the church of every time and place. Our common baptism, which unites us to Christ in faith, is thus a basic bond of unity. The union with Christ which we share through baptism has important implications for Christian unity" (B6). According to the Second Vatican Council, by the sacrament of baptism one "becomes truly incorporated into the crucified and glorified Christ... Baptism, therefore, constitutes a sacramental bond of unity linking all who have been reborn by means of it" (*Unitatis Redintegratio [UR]* 22 1964).

6. On the other hand, Faith and Order's evaluation of the official responses to BEM 1990 noted areas where further study should be undertaken on baptism. A comparison of some of the specific responses to BEM indicate that there are still important issues that need to be resolved in dialogue among the churches before we can speak of a genuinely common understanding of baptism. Furthermore, some new problems are emerging which need to be addressed lest the convergence/consensus achieved be somehow diminished (see §109 below).

A MORE RECENT ECUMENICAL CHALLENGE:

7. In addition, another significant ecumenical challenge arises from among the fastest growing and largest Christian communities today, Pentecostals and Evangelicals, many of whom have not been directly involved in the modern ecumenical movement. A particular challenge that they bring is that many of these Christians do not see baptism itself as the point of entry into the body of Christ, but rather as an intimately related consequence of that entry.[1] The growth of communities with this viewpoint presents a new ecumenical challenge for today and the future.

THE PRESENT STUDY

8. Despite these various challenges, the creation of a new relationship among separated Christians has been an ecumenical achievement. The purpose of this study is to help the churches to build on this accomplishment and, in particular, on the contribution made to the unity of Christians by the growing acknowledgment of a common baptism. This text reviews some fundamental aspects of the degree of the current ecumenical convergences and consensus on baptism while also pointing to differences still remaining. Thus, one can speak of a "common" baptism in a legitimate, though qualified, sense. On

the one hand, the degree of common understanding of baptism which has been achieved ecumenically has already been a building block for unity and has already helped to create new relationships and foster reconciliation between separated Christians. On the other hand, further ecumenical work on baptism is still needed to resolve continuing difficulties if further progress is to be made.

9. This study points also to some of the implications, ecclesiological and ecumenical, of a common baptism for the goal of unity which we seek.[2] *Ecclesiological implications* refer to issues relating to the doctrine of the church and thus inter-related with baptism. They concern those remaining theological divergences among Christians which now more urgently need to be resolved, or to which more ecumenical attention must now be given in order to take further steps towards a common understanding of the church and the healing of divisions among Christians. These will be noted in each specific section. *Ecumenical implications* refer to those practical, pastoral steps that might be taken now to implement the growing common understanding of baptism. They are steps based on the degree of communion Christians already share, and therefore may also have an ecclesial character – steps that can help separated Christians to grow together. These are listed in the section 6 at the end.

10. This is a study document meant to enable discussion. It is the hope of the Joint Working Group that this study will be used in educational contexts in which ecumenical matters are explored. It is hoped that this study can assist and encourage the Catholic Church and the member churches of the WCC to open a discussion on ecclesial and ecumenical implications of the recognition of a common baptism and to take appropriate steps to manifest a greater degree of communion.

1. Growing ecumenical convergence on baptism

11. From the beginning of the modern ecumenical movement baptism has been claimed as a common bond for Christians and has been the subject of intensive conversation among the churches. In this section and in the pages that follow some of the basic convergences on baptism achieved in dialogue are recalled. The differences that still remain are presented as well in order to indicate the further work that needs to be done.

COMMON PERSPECTIVES ON BAPTISM

12. Through shared study churches have discovered common perspectives on baptism relating to (a) its foundational place in the church, (b) the primary aspects of its meaning, and (c) the pattern or *ordo* of elements in the process of baptismal initiation. They have also made notable steps in bringing closer the views of baptism as *sacrament* and baptism as *ordinance*.

13. The ecumenical convergence and agreements on baptism found in BEM mark an important step forward in the ecumenical movement. Many of the official responses from member churches of the World Council of Churches found much to praise in the baptism section of BEM. The response of the Catholic Church to that baptism section (*Churches Respond to BEM*, vol. 6, WCC, 1988, pp. 9-16) was largely affirmative, finding "much we can agree with", while, as many other responses, raising issues in need of further study. Important clarifications on baptism have been made in bilateral dialogues as well.

14. Ecumenical study has enabled separated Christians to appreciate together the *priority of the liturgical act of baptism*. In faithful obedience to the great commission from the risen Christ (Matt. 28:19-20, "Go therefore and make disciples of all nations, baptizing them in the name of the Father and of the Son and of the Holy Spirit, and teaching them everything I have commanded you"), the church's practice of baptism responds to the apostolic calling to preach the gospel and make disciples. From the beginning, baptism was part of the mission of the apostolic church and its practice was part of the constitution of the church. Before there was an established canon of the New Testament scriptures and while the ecclesial structure was still developing, baptism was a constitutive element of Christian life. As an act of repentance, forgiveness, profession, incorporation and eschatological hope, the observance of baptism recapitulates and embodies the reality of the church, which continually lives out these same relations with God through Christ in its worship, sacraments, teaching, *koinonia* and service. As a specific rite, baptism anchors a wider complex of steps in the initiation, growth and identity of individual believers within the body of Christ. But baptism is not only an event for individuals and a bond of unity among Christians. As such, it is also one expression and icon of the church's very nature.

15. Despite variations in baptismal practice that existed within an undivided church (as for instance variations in the local baptismal creeds that were used), ecumenical dialogue has enabled separated Christians to identify the shared pattern of the early church *as a common heritage* for the divided churches today, being the foundation of the understanding and practice of baptism in each Christian communion. In that common heritage "baptism is administered with water in the name of the Father, the Son and the Holy Spirit" (B17). "In baptism a profession of faith is given according to the Trinitarian content of the faith of the community *(regula fidei)*." This "baptismal confession joins the faith of the baptized to the common faith of the church through the ages" (*Confessing the One Faith*, introduction, 15).

16. "The New Testament scriptures and the liturgy of the church unfold the meaning of baptism in various images which express the riches of Christ and the gifts of his salvation" (BEM 2). Reflecting this heritage, *Baptism, Eucharist and Ministry* (B3-7) identifies five major sets of images: (a) participation in Christ's death and resurrection; (b) conversion, pardoning and cleansing; (c) gift of the Spirit; (d) incorporation into the body of Christ; and (e) sign of the kingdom. While ecumenical convergence can be claimed on these points, the need for further work can be illustrated by looking at point (d). While BEM states that "our common baptism... is a basic bond of unity" (B6) and that baptism is "incorporation into the body of Christ" (B comm. 14b), there are different views relating to that incorporation which reflect unresolved differences in ecclesiology. Thus, many would agree that incorporation in the church is through baptism, but some responses to BEM indicate that full incorporation into the church, the body of Christ, implies not just baptism, but rather a larger process of Christian initiation of which baptism is a part. The reality of new life in Jesus Christ and rebirth in the Holy Spirit is described in BEM with a wide variety of spiritual images. Christian traditions have differed in the weight they give to these images in understanding baptism. The churches can all be enriched by learning from each other in order to grasp the breadth of the meaning of baptism.

17. Many of the convergences in these areas are reflected in results of bilateral dialogues which also point to areas where further discussion is needed. To give two examples, the Anglican-Reformed International Commission report "God's Reign and Our Unity" (1984 §§47-61) reflects BEM's convergences. But differences appear when the text discusses the related question of membership. Reformed churches have tended to define it "primarily as membership in a local congregation", while Anglicans, "by practice of episcopal confirmation, have emphasized membership in the wider church". The report states that these emphases "are complementary rather than contradictory", but "require further exploration by our churches" (§57). The international Catholic-Orthodox dialogue reflects BEM's convergences in its list of seven points of agreement ("Faith, Sacraments and the Unity of the Church", 1987, §49). However, the latter also includes important areas of agreement between Orthodox and Catholics which are not as explicitly stated in BEM, e.g., the "necessity of baptism for salvation", and as an effect of baptism, the "liberation from original sin" *(ibid.)*.

18. In current ecumenical discussion three dimensions of the common pattern of baptism are noted – three distinct ways to understand the scope of this pattern. First of all, in the most basic sense, baptism refers to the liturgical water rite and the pattern for its celebration. Second, baptism may also refer to a wider pattern of Christian initiation, one that includes several components in addition to the specific liturgical rite of baptism. In a third sense, we may see that baptism points towards ongoing formation and responsible discipleship, where the pattern of our baptismal calling is worked out over a whole life. With the first perspective in view, we could say that baptism is one of the elements that make up the life of the church. With the third perspective in view, we could say that the baptismal pattern marks the entire life of believers in the church.

19. "Baptism is related not only to momentary experience, but to life-long growth into Christ" (BEM 9). In the early church this was expressed in the emergence of complex patterns of Christian nurture which included instruction in the faith before and after baptism, as well as an extended series of liturgical celebrations marking the journey in a growing faith. These aspects were focused in the water rite of baptism and admission to the eucharistic table. In its broadest sense the ordo (or pattern) of baptism includes formation in faith, baptism in water, and participation in the life of the community. In different Christian traditions the order and expression of these aspects varies.

20. The ecumenical and ecclesial consequences of agreement about baptism vary greatly, depending upon which dimension of this common pattern is in view. The churches have a high degree of agreement about the fundamental components of the liturgical water rite and its necessity. As the pattern is expanded, the specific agreement among the churches diminishes. For example, there are fewer disputes about recognition of baptism centred on whether the rite has been performed with water in the name of Father, Son and Holy Spirit, than relate to the place of the rite in this larger pattern of initiation or formation.

SACRAMENT AND ORDINANCE

21. Many churches use the term sacrament to express their understanding of what the common pattern or ordo of baptism is. Some churches are uncomfortable with the notion of sacrament and they prefer to speak of baptism as an ordinance. A brief look at

the history of these two terms may help to identify the issue and suggest that it may not be as divisive as is sometimes thought.

22. When the Greek fathers used the word *musterion* to describe baptism, and when the Latins translated this by *mysterium* or *sacramentum* they wanted to say that, in the celebration of baptism, the saving work of God in Christ is realized by the power of the Holy Spirit. In the Latin church *sacramentum* (from which comes our modern word sacrament) came to be a generic term applied to baptism and eucharist, as well as to some other rites of the church. A sacrament was understood to be a symbolic action, made up of words and actions which held within it and manifested the divine reality *(res)* realized once for all in the death and resurrection of Christ for our salvation. This notion of sacrament was very carefully analyzed in Scholastic theology. Some elements of the analysis, however, lent themselves to misunderstanding, especially when they were associated with forms of liturgical practice that seemed to encourage belief in a quasi-mechanical view of sacramental efficacy, as if sacraments dispensed grace in an automatic way.

23. The word "ordinance" stresses that certain acts within the worship and liturgy of the church are performed in obedience to the specific command and example of Christ in scripture. Those who use the term "sacraments" usually also regard them as ordinances in this sense. Historically, some Christian groups adopted "ordinance" language in the Reformation era because of arguments over whether certain liturgical acts were actually instituted by Christ in scripture and because of their rejection of certain theological views about the working of God's grace which they believed were involved in the definition of "sacraments". Some churches which use only the word "ordinance" regard acts such as baptism and the Lord's supper as signs of a reality that has already been actualized and which is even now effective by faith in the life of the believer and the congregation. Some who use only the word "ordinance" would in fact give this a "sacramental" meaning, consistent with the explanation of sacraments in churches that use the term. Those who characterize baptism as an ordinance wish to safeguard an understanding of its root in scripture, its confessional character as witness to Christ, and the initiative of God, active to stir faith and conversion in the believer prior to baptism. This view has often wrongly been construed as denying that God is active in the event of baptism or that God's grace is received in baptism; in fact, it is an attempt to affirm the faithful act of discipleship through participation in baptism, the centrality of Christ to the act of baptism and the breadth of God's grace already active in our lives prior to, as well as in, baptism.

24. This divergent language is in some cases based on misunderstanding, but in other instances on disagreement which remains, even after clarification. Nevertheless, most traditions can agree that the realities in the church's life called sacraments or ordinances bring Christians to the central mysteries of life in Christ. Most would affirm of ordinances/sacraments both that they are expressive of divine realities, representing that which is already true, and also that they are instrumental in that God uses them to bring about a new reality. The two approaches represent different starting points in considering the interdependence of faith as an ongoing process and faith as a decisive event. At other points in this document further areas of convergence are explored, for instance in the discussion of the relation of baptism and faith in section 3.

THE ECUMENICAL IMPACT OF THE GROWING CONVERGENCE ON BAPTISM

25. While there is not yet a complete agreement on baptism among separated Christians, the growing convergence that has been achieved thus far can be counted among the important achievements of the modern ecumenical movement. As the following examples illustrate, this growing convergence has already been able to serve the cause of reconciliation, fostering unity between different churches in different ways. This is one sense in which the growing consensus on baptism even now has ecclesiological implications.

26. Ecumenical agreements bringing some churches into new relationships, in some cases even into full communion, include mutual understanding of baptism as part of their theological basis. The Leuenberg agreement (1973) between Lutheran and Reformed churches in Europe includes, as part of "The Common Understanding of the Gospel" needed for church fellowship among them, a basic consensus regarding baptism (§14), even though the agreement indicates that the question of "baptismal practice" needs further study (§39). The nine member churches of the Churches Uniting in Christ (2001) in the United States have included in their theological consensus the convergences and agreements on baptism found in *Baptism, Eucharist and Ministry*.

27. In several ecumenical advances which have taken place involving the Catholic Church with Christian world communions which include member churches of the WCC, a common understanding of baptism has been crucial. In their common declaration at Canterbury in 1982, Pope John Paul II and Archbishop of Canterbury Dr Robert Runcie stated that "the bond of our common baptism into Christ" led their predecessors to inaugurate the international dialogue between the Anglican Communion and the Catholic Church. The same two leaders in their common declaration in Rome in 1989 stated that the "certain yet incomplete communion we already share" is grounded in sharing together important areas of faith including "our common baptism into Christ".

28. The Joint Declaration on the Doctrine of Justification (JD), officially signed by the Catholic Church and the Lutheran World Federation (1999), expresses an agreement on basic truths of the doctrine of justification. It is historic in stating that the teaching of the Lutheran churches and the Catholic Church presented in the declaration are not subject to the condemnations of the other's teaching found respectively in the council of Trent and in the Lutheran confessions in the 16th century. The JD's explication of justification comes in seven core areas, in two of which baptism is central. In §25 we read, "We confess together that sinners are justified by faith in the saving action of God in Christ. By the action of the Holy Spirit in baptism, they are granted the gift of salvation, which lays the basis for the whole Christian life." And in §28, "We confess together that in baptism the Holy Spirit unites one with Christ, justifies and truly renews the person."

29. In several joint declarations between the pope and patriarchs of Oriental Orthodox churches, reflecting resolution of long-standing problems, agreement on baptism has also been an important factor. For example, the joint declaration between Pope John Paul II and Syrian Orthodox Patriarch Mar Ignatius Zakka I Iwas (1984) expresses agreement on Christology in a way which virtually resolves for them the Christological conflicts arising from the doctrinal formulations of the council of Chalcedon (451). The agreement also describes common perspectives today on baptism, eucharist and other sacraments, and a common understanding of sacraments which they hold together "in

one and the same succession of apostolic ministry" (§7). This allows them to authorize collaboration in pastoral care in situations where their faithful find access to a priest of their own church "materially or morally impossible". Nonetheless, at the same time, they say that their churches cannot celebrate the holy eucharist together since that supposes a complete identity of faith, including a common understanding of God's will for the church, which does not yet exist between them.

ECCLESIOLOGICAL IMPLICATIONS

30. Many other examples could be cited that illustrate the impact of the growing convergence on baptism. But what has been said thus far in this first section suggests several *ecclesiological implications* of a common baptism. *First*, a common baptism is among those factors which have enabled, even inspired, some long separated churches to enter into new relationships with one another. Some of these are significant new relationships, but not of full communion. Others are relationships of full communion, or, as in the case of those participating in the Leuenberg Agreement, of pulpit and altar fellowship.

31. *Second*, those Christian communities which agree that baptism means incorporation into the body of Christ, the church, and who agree that the church is one, should belong to one and the same community. If there is one church of Jesus Christ and if baptism is entrance into it, then all those who are baptized are bound to one another in Christ and should be in full communion with one another. There should not be a division among ecclesial communities; baptism should impel Christians to work for the elimination of divisions.

32. It also follows that even if there is agreement on a common understanding of baptism, churches nonetheless differ concerning what they require for achieving full communion with those from whom they are separated. This is because they have divergent understandings of the nature of the church. Thus, a *third* ecclesiological implication of a common understanding of baptism, from what has been described above, is the urgency within the ecumenical movement of working towards a common understanding of the nature of the church. This is important so that, as new relationships take shape among some churches, the agreements that bind them together will include perspectives on the nature of the church which would be open to reconciliation with other churches in the future as the ecumenical movement progresses.

33. *Fourth*, since baptism is foundational for the nature of the church, then it is one of the prerequisites for full communion. If a particular Christian community does not celebrate baptism, then its members are without one of the important elements which make for communion with all other baptized Christians. The level of communion between such a community and the communities who celebrate baptism is significantly impaired.

2.   Baptism and initiation into the life of faith

34. When the gospel is preached and the call to conversion is heard, a process of incorporation into life in Christ is set in motion in the one who is called to salvation (Acts 2:37-42). While the process continues throughout life until the Christian is definitively incorporated into Christ at the parousia, its earthly course is marked by certain

decisive moments, in which significant stages of life in Christ are first realized and manifested. These moments taken together can be called Christian initiation. They are moments of faith and conversion, of ritual celebration and of entry into the life of the church. Baptism is at the heart of the process, both as decisive moment and as model of the entire process.

35. The churches are united in confessing that "there is one Lord, one faith, one baptism" (Eph. 4:5). United in the one Lord, they affirm that faith and baptism belong together. They can agree that faith calls for baptism, and that the rite of baptism expresses the faith of the church of Christ and of the person baptized. Baptism expresses faith in the gracious gift of God that justifies sinners; it celebrates the realization of that gift in a new member of the church. This faith is handed on in the church, in its life and teaching, and is appropriated as the faith of the church by the person baptized.

THE RITES OF CHRISTIAN INITIATION

36. Christian initiation is effected in a complex interplay of faith and conversion, of ritual celebration, of teaching and spiritual formation, of practice and of mission. While there are differences between churches in the way the relationship between these elements is understood, there is widespread agreement that the water-rite of baptism is at the heart of initiation.

37. "Baptism is administered with water in the name of the Father, the Son and the Holy Spirit" (B17). The baptismal rite has taken different forms in the history of the church's life. While churches have their individual normative practices, they often recognize other forms as constituting a true baptism. On the one hand, total or partial immersion of the candidate in water seems to be the form best grounded in the Tradition, and to be acceptable to most churches. Many recognize as true a baptism that is done by the pouring of water on the person, particularly on the head. On the other hand various churches doubt whether a sprinkling with water is a sufficient sacramental sign. More ecumenically problematic is the practice of some churches, noted by BEM, that have a rite of initiation that does not use water but is nevertheless called baptism (comm. 21c). Most difficult to reconcile with the understanding of most Christians concerning baptism and the church are the procedures for initiation into Christian faith and life of some Christian communities that lack any specific rite resembling baptism and even deliberately exclude baptism.

38. In many churches chrismation/confirmation and first reception of the eucharist are associated with baptism as rites of initiation. While there are differences in the way the relationship between these three rites is understood and practised in the churches, and their bearing on Christian life is not always experienced in the same way, it is generally accepted that they give expression and reality to different aspects of a single process of initiation. Baptism is intrinsically related to the other two rites, in so far as it calls forth the gift of the eschatological Spirit and brings one into communion in the body of Christ; they, for their part, are grounded in baptism and draw meaning from it.

39. Some churches do not practise chrismation/confirmation, and others who do so allow reception of the eucharist before chrismation/confirmation. While these practices are problematical for other churches they do not call into question the fundamental orientation of baptism to eucharist and its role as precondition for receiving the eucharist to which the whole Christian Tradition bears witness.

40. The sacrament of baptism is, in the first meaning of the term, a distinctive water-rite that occurs once in a life-time and cannot be repeated. The ongoing gift of growth in faith and the continual dying and rising in Christ that this entails is truly a living out of the once-for-all encounter of faith with Christ that is given and modelled in the rite of baptism. In this sense Christian life can be understood as a "life-long baptism", lasting until final oneness with Christ is attained.

BAPTISM AND FAITH

41. Baptism as rite, and as a daily dying and rising with Christ, is inseparable from faith. God, who calls persons by name (Isa. 43:1; cf. Acts 9:4), is the source of faith. Even the freedom to respond in faith is God's gracious gift. Faith begins in persons when God sows in them the seed of simple trust. By the witness of the Holy Spirit they grow up into Christ, in whom the fullness of God dwells (Col. 1:19). It is not on the basis of their own understanding or ability that human beings can receive God's gift, but only through the grace of our Lord Jesus Christ (Rom. 3:24; 1 Cor. 1:26ff.). Nothing can be claimed for baptism that would interfere with the utter gratuitousness of the gift of God received in faith.

42. Faith is the response of the believer to the gospel of salvation in Jesus Christ, preached in and by the community of those who already believe in him and praise the glory of his name. Drawn into that faith, the new believer gradually makes his/her own the words in which the gospel of salvation is expressed. These are primarily the words of the scriptures, and particularly the confessions of faith that they contain. They are also those symbols of faith, those distillations of the gospel, that the churches have recognized as expressions of the faith and authorized for use in worship and teaching. It is these words of faith, crystallized in the Trinitarian formula "in the name of the Father and of the Son and of the Holy Spirit", that give form and meaning to the water rite of baptism and that in the early church led to it being called sacrament of faith.

43. Thus baptism situates the faith of the Christian within the living faith of the church and so contributes to the growth of his or her faith. "As Christians mature, they grow up into the fullness of the faith confessed, celebrated and witnessed to by the Christian community, both locally and worldwide... in the faith professed by the whole church throughout the ages... The 'we believe' of the Christian community and the 'I believe' of personal commitment become one" (second Faith and Order consultation on baptism at Faverges, 2001, 48).

44. The Trinitarian faith confessed in the baptismal creed and the baptismal washing performed by the church in the name of the Father, Son and Holy Spirit are indissolubly united in the liturgy of holy baptism. In the creed the church testifies to its faith in the Triune God, and incorporates those baptized into God's holy people. This connection between the baptismal formula and the believing church is at the core of the process of Christian initiation. In this sense baptism is always understood to be believer's baptism.

45. The faith confessed in baptism is the faith that binds believers and their churches together. In early centuries Christian communities shared their baptismal creeds as a basis of unity. Later, councils expressed the same faith in more extensive formulations. The heart of the faith expressed in the most universally acknowledged creeds used today – the Nicene-Constantinopolitan and the Apostles Creeds – is the faith in the

Triune God, Father, Son and Holy Spirit. And "the profession of faith occurs also in those churches which do not formally use the words of the Nicene Creed, when baptismal confession uses other formulas authorized by the church" (*Confessing the One Faith*, introduction, §15).

46. Churches that share faith in the Trinity and fully recognize one another's baptism may, nevertheless, break communion with each other due to differences about other matters of faith or questions of order. In this case the communion which is the fruit of faith and baptism is impeded. There are churches which consider that a disagreement in faith that is sufficiently serious to be communion-breaking between them and another church makes them unable to admit baptized members of that church to full participation in the eucharist, the normal fulfillment of baptism. Many other churches, however, consider that, even in the absence of full ecclesial communion, churches should admit members of other churches, whose baptism they recognize and Trinitarian faith they share, to full participation in the eucharist.

ADULT BAPTISM AND THE BAPTISM OF INFANTS

47. Most churches can share the broad understanding of the relation between faith and baptism that has been described above. But differences remain which lead to problems for the mutual recognition of baptism. The differences are not very apparent when the baptism being considered is that of an adult. Two facts provide a unifying point of reference for churches regarding the manner and meaning of the baptism of adults. First, biblical descriptions of the pattern of initiation normally refer to adults. Second, major classical liturgies of baptism were initially intended for adults. Such baptisms, celebrated according to the present-day rituals and disciplines of almost all churches, are normally the baptism of actual believers, and can be recognized as such. But when baptism is administered to a child who is not yet capable of making a personal profession of faith, the interpretation of the scriptural and traditional material on baptism can differ. For some churches the scriptures only authorize the baptizing of those who make a personal act of conversion and a personal confession of faith. For others the scriptures provide no compelling reason for refusing baptism to children not yet capable of such personal decisions, when they are presented by those who are responsible for them and are entrusted by them to the church for their formation and instruction. Furthermore, descriptions in Acts of the baptism of whole households must be taken carefully into account. And, even though classical baptismal liturgies were designed for adults, a very early and extensive description of such a liturgy, the *Apostolic Tradition* of Hippolytus (c.215), explicitly includes the initiation of children who cannot answer for themselves (XX, 4).

48. It must be recognized with BEM that "the necessity of faith for the reception of the salvation embodied and set forth in baptism is acknowledged by the churches. Personal commitment is necessary for responsible membership in the body of Christ" (B8). "While the possibility that infant baptism was also practised in the apostolic age cannot be excluded, baptism upon personal profession of faith is the most clearly attested pattern in the New Testament documents" (B11). The churches recognize the paradigmatic and normative quality of the baptism of adult believers, illustrated in the New Testament and practised by all churches, as the most explicit sign of the character of baptism. However, as BEM goes on to note, "In the course of history, the practice of

baptism has developed in a variety of forms. Some churches baptize infants brought by parents or guardians who are ready, in and with the church, to bring up the children in the Christian faith. Other churches practise exclusively the baptism of believers who are able to make a personal confession of faith. Some of these churches encourage infants or children to be presented and blessed in a service which usually involves thanksgiving for the gift of the child and also the commitment of the mother and father to Christian parenthood" (B11).

49.   It has to be noted here that the development of infant baptism is rooted in the history of the early church and was never intended to be a departure from the pattern of initiation that we have identified and that is ordained in the New Testament texts on baptism. Children were baptized because God's call to salvation seemed to bear on them no less than on adults. Age could be no barrier to the gift of God in Christ and the Spirit. In the celebration of baptism the rite was always associated with faith and with life in the community of believers. In infants, faith took the form of the living faith of the church that gathered the child to itself in baptism. The faith of the church was understood to be now present in this new member in the form of the faith-nurture that was henceforth enfolding it. Faith was understood to be an already-present grace that would enable the child to grow up to the point of being able to make a personal confession of faith and personally ratify the grace of conversion that had been given in baptism. The ground of this conviction was the understanding that the grace of Christ has taken hold of all the children of Adam and can free them from sin once they are brought into contact with him through the preaching and sacraments of the church. It is only and always this grace that generates the human response that is inherent to faith. It can be already at work in the nurture through which children are being brought to the point of being able to make personal choices.

50.   Churches that practise only the baptism of adult believers are no less caring for children than the churches that baptize them. They also welcome children for instruction, care and blessing within the community. They mark the commitment of Christian parents and their ecclesial community (and in some cases of specific sponsors as well) to nurture a newborn child in the faith, within the life of the church. Even though the welcome is not enacted through baptism it looks towards baptism as its horizon. For people so welcomed into the church in childhood, baptism in adult age can be the personal expression of the climax of a journey of conversion and faith, which is one of the principle ways in which the scriptures speak of it. Furthermore, the ecumenical convergence being reached about the sacramental status of baptism can now enable churches that baptize only those who can make a personal act of faith to see the baptism they administer as also embodying the grace of Christ and the gift of the Spirit that brings about the personal faith and conversion that is expressed in the celebration.

51.   In the Latin tradition infant baptism received strong support in the theology of Augustine and his reaction against Pelagian views. This view gave expression to the fear of exposing infants to the danger of dying without being rescued from [original] sin by the saving work of Christ, as well as to the positive advantages of initiation into life in Christ and his church that baptism brings. A restored theology of baptism and a critical re-evaluation of certain explanations of the consequences of original sin for children would give increased weight to the Christological and ecclesiological reality of baptism. These churches also recognize that there are risks of mishandling the gifts of God in

baptizing children. The promises of Christian nurture given by parents and sponsors may not be kept and the sacrament may be profaned. In fact, these churches have, theoretically if not always in practice, required that baptism be delayed until the child is old enough to speak for him/herself when there is not a reasonable guarantee that the child will be nurtured in the faith. While these concerns, which must surely be intensified in our post-Christian world, do not amount to identifying with the position of churches that practise only believer's baptism, they certainly indicate a belief that the full pattern of Christian initiation must be respected. In this they affirm something that can serve as an important ground for recognition of baptism between them and churches that practise only believer's baptism.

52. We have proposed that the pattern of baptismal initiation has three elements: formation in faith, baptism in water, and participation in the life of the community. These three elements are present in the rite of water baptism itself for every church, though not in the same way. Likewise all three elements are present in the life-long process of Christian discipleship, with its continual formation in faith, recollection of baptismal grace and promise, and deepening participation in the life of the church. If we ask about the relation of faith to baptism in reference to the water rite alone, the differences among the churches remain substantial. When we compare instead the wider pattern of baptismal initiation and formation in Christ, more extensive convergence emerges. It is a convergence that is compatible with and even enriched by the fact that different traditions emphasize one or other element of the pattern and put them together in different ways.

53. The convergence is grounded on the fact that churches recognize a paradigmatic and normative quality of baptism performed upon personal profession of faith, illustrated in the New Testament and practised by all churches, as the most explicit sign of the character of baptism. Those traditions that practise only this form of baptism in their pattern of initiation maintain a living witness to the reality of baptism the churches affirm together, and express powerfully the shared conviction that baptism is inherently oriented to personal conversion. Those traditions that practise infant baptism as part of their pattern of initiation maintain a living witness to the initiating call and grace from God that the churches agree enable human response, and express powerfully the shared convictions that infants and children are nurtured and received within the community of Christ's church prior to any explicit confession.

54. It is being suggested that each church, even as it retains its own baptismal tradition, recognize in others the one baptism into Jesus Christ by affirming the similarity of wider patterns of initiation and formation in Christ present in every community. This is the convergence foreseen in *Baptism, Eucharist and Ministry*: "Churches are increasingly recognizing one another's baptism as the one baptism into Christ, when Jesus Christ has been confessed as Lord by the candidate or, in the case of infant baptism, when confession has been made by the church (parents, guardians, godparents and congregation) and affirmed later by personal faith and commitment" (B15). Those churches that practise only believer's baptism could recognize the one baptism in other traditions within their full patterns of Christian initiation, which include personal affirmation of faith. Those churches that normally practise infant baptism could recognize the one baptism within the full pattern of Christian initiation in "believer's churches", even where identical forms of chrismation or confirmation were lacking.

55. Recognition that the one baptism of Christ is present within another tradition's full pattern of Christian initiation can also reinforce another key affirmation in *Baptism, Eucharist and Ministry*: "Baptism is an unrepeatable act. Any practice which might be interpreted as 're-baptism' must be avoided" (B13).

ECCLESIOLOGICAL IMPLICATIONS

56. There is an intimate relationship between baptism and faith. This, and the fact that the various churches in their baptismal practice have the intent to baptize into the universal body of Christ (cf. §42), but in fact baptize into communities separated from one another, often because of serious differences in their understanding of aspects of Christian faith, suggests the following. *An ecclesiological implication of the emerging convergence on baptism is that this development makes more urgent the achievement, by separated Christians, of a common understanding of the apostolic faith which the church proclaims and in light of which a person is baptized.*

57. Concerning the disagreement about baptizing infants, those on both sides agree that baptism is related to personal faith. One position holds that personal faith is a condition for being baptized, and the other that personal faith is required of the person baptized as soon as it becomes possible. But a significant difference between the two positions concerns the role taken by the church, as suggested in statements above explaining infant baptism: "In infants, faith took the form of the living faith of the church that gathered the child to itself in baptism" (§49); faith was understood as "an already-present grace that would enable the child to grow up…able to make its personal confession of faith and personally ratify the grace of conversion… given in baptism…," a conviction based on the understanding "… that the grace of Christ has taken hold of all the children of Adam and can free them from sin once they are brought into contact with him through the preaching and sacraments of the church" (§49). *The ecclesiological implication which follows is that among the basic issues which need to be resolved in order to overcome the divergence on infant baptism are the questions of the nature and purpose of the church and its role in the economy of salvation.*

3. Baptism and incorporation into the church

58. Both the rite of baptism, as well as the life-long process of growing into Christ which it initiates, take place within a particular (local) church community. Its members and ministers preach the gospel, invite, instruct and ritually prepare its catechumens, celebrate the sacramental rites of initiation, register the act and take responsibility for the ongoing Christian formation and sacramental completion of those baptized in it. Such a baptizing community believes that the one, holy, catholic and apostolic church of Christ is realized in itself. Thus the baptism it celebrates is the gift of the Spirit that incorporates the baptized, at one and the same time, into its own community life and into the body of Christ that is his church. The communion which this local church has with other churches expresses and embodies the oneness of Christians that is given in the body of Christ. The eucharist, as the sacrament of the body and blood of Christ given for the salvation of all, brings the communion given in baptism to its sacramental fullness.

59. All churches agree that the incorporation into Christ that is inaugurated in baptism is intended to be, as gift of Christ in the Spirit to the glory of God the Father, complete and full incorporation. Correspondingly, baptism expresses the intention to admit the baptized person into the universal communion of the church of Christ. Christian communities do not baptize into themselves as isolated units but as churches that believe the body of Christ is present and available in their own ecclesial reality. The desire for communion in the body of Christ inherent in baptism compels the baptized to reach out to other ecclesial communities that practise the same pattern of baptism and confess the same apostolic faith.

60. When the communities that baptize are in full communion with each other – as when they already belong to the same ecclesial family – communion between their members is sacramentally and institutionally completed and its spiritual fruitfulness is correspondingly enhanced. The baptized together share the same eucharist, in which communion is fully expressed and nourished. They live together with the same faith, and the same institutional bonds of mission, ministry and service.

61. When there are obstacles to full communion among different communities, baptism still provides a degree of communion that is real, if imperfect. The baptized can recognize in the baptismal faith and practice of those others a belief in and desire for the oneness of Christians in the body of Christ that corresponds to their own. They can recognize in one another's baptism a visible and institutional expression of the unity in Christ into which the members of each church believe they have been baptized and find in that an expression and nourishment of their desire for the ecclesial fullness of that unity.

62. Nor do the difficulties that some churches have about recognizing the full sacramental reality of baptism celebrated in churches not in full communion with themselves – difficulties that have to be recognized and respected – deprive baptism of all significance for communion. The position of the Orthodox is a case in point. There is a complication when a non-Orthodox wishes to join the Orthodox church, as baptism, chrismation/confirmation and the eucharist are considered to be *one* sacrament of initiation. As a result, practices vary. Baptism is used if the postulant is deemed not to be baptized in the name of the Holy Trinity (e.g. Unitarians). Chrismation is performed in the case of absence of confirmation, or in the case of a different conception of confirmation. But in the case, for instance, of a Roman Catholic, the reception should be performed through confession and communion, recognizing and respecting the holy orders and the full sacramentality of the Roman Catholic Church. This, for example, is the *official* attitude of the church of Russia among others. However, among the Orthodox, a difficulty arises from the fact that there exists a difference between Orthodox theology which recognizes baptism in the name of the Holy Trinity, and the practice of some Orthodox communities – not churches – e.g. Mount Athos, that rebaptize non-Orthodox Christians (Mount Athos is part of the church of Constantinople which follows Orthodox theology as described above).

63. Some churches do not admit to eucharistic communion all those whose baptism they recognize. But according to Roman Catholic theology, the desire *(votum)* for the eucharist is given in every true baptism, and the reality *(res)* of grace – union with Christ – is acknowledged to exist because of baptism even when access to eucharistic communion is denied or restricted (see also §§92-95 below).

CONFIRMATION AND OTHER SACRAMENTS

64. The relation of baptism and other sacraments, especially confirmation, needs further discussion. The convergence text BEM (B14) states, "In God's work of salvation, the paschal mystery of Christ's death and resurrection is inseparably linked with the pentecostal gift of the Holy Spirit. Similarly, participation in Christ's death and resurrection is inseparably linked with the receiving of the Spirit. Baptism in its full meaning signifies and effects both."

65. But the differences might be outlined in this way. In some churches confirmation has its origins in a post-baptismal episcopal anointing or imposition of hands in early Christianity – an event which, in the course of history in the West, became separated in time from the baptismal ritual [in the East, chrismation/confirmation, being delegated to the priest by the bishop, is part of the baptismal ceremony]. In other churches, particularly Reformation churches, confirmation means a more mature profession of faith by adolescents. Thus for certain traditions confirmation is a sacramental part of the baptismal action (even if performed years later). For most traditions confirmation is understood as "completing" baptism. For some traditions, however, confirmation is a distinctive sacramental rite understood not as "completing" a person's earlier baptism – *that* is viewed as complete in and of itself – but as an act by a person, now "mature", that publicly witnesses to and affirms it (cf. Faith and Order consultation, Faverges, October 2001, no. 26).

66. Christians differ, then, in their understanding as to where the sign of the gift of the Spirit is to be found. Different actions have become associated with the giving of the Spirit. For some it is the water rite itself. For others, it is the anointing with chrism and/or the imposition of hands, which many churches call confirmation. For still others it is all three, as they see the Spirit operative throughout the rite. All agree that Christian baptism is in water and the Holy Spirit. But the place and role of confirmation within the practice of Christian initiation needs further clarification among the churches.

ECCLESIOLOGICAL IMPLICATIONS

67. This discussion on "baptism and incorporation into the church" suggests several ecclesiological implications. *First, the implication of the common belief that baptism is incorporation into the body of Christ, the church, is that the rite of baptism is an effective sign which really accomplishes something in the life of the person who receives it.*

68. But, despite this common belief just mentioned, there are also different convictions among Christians governing the way they understand various theological aspects of baptism, or the sacramental aspect of incorporation, or indeed the sacraments themselves. For some, incorporation into the church comes through the sacraments of initiation which include baptism, confirmation and eucharist. For others, the celebration of the sacrament of baptism alone suffices for incorporation into the body of Christ. For still others, it is a profession of faith in Jesus Christ which brings one into the church, and baptism is a sign of acknowledgment that this has taken place. *In light of these differences, a second ecclesiological implication from the discussion of this aspect of the emerging convergence on baptism is the need to develop common ecumenical perspectives on the sacraments, and especially on the relationship of sacraments to the church.*

69. Also, there are different evaluations of the nature of confirmation and its status as a sacrament. *A third implication follows, namely that it would be valuable for disagreeing communities to dialogue about the precise question of whether this difference concerning confirmation reflects any ecclesiological disagreement.*

4. Baptism and continual growth in Christ

70. As previously pointed out, one of the dimensions of the common pattern of baptism is the "ongoing formation and responsible discipleship where the pattern of our baptismal calling is worked out over a whole life" (see above 18). Whatever the age of the person, in fact, baptism marks the beginning of a new life in Christ and in the church, and this life is characterized by growth. The Christian life, based on and nourished by faith, involves becoming more and more what God promises and creates in baptism. Life in Christ is life in the Holy Spirit who guides and empowers us to fulfil our baptismal vocation which is to participate in the *missio Dei*, being realized in the ongoing history of salvation.

GROWTH IN CHRIST

71. Christian life is not characterized only by growth. Rather, the baptismal participation in Christ's death and resurrection includes, also, the need for daily repentance and forgiveness. Life in Christ therefore involves a readiness to forgive just as we have been forgiven, thus opening the baptized to attitudes and behaviours that shape a new ethical orientation. According to BEM: "... those baptized are pardoned, cleansed and sanctified by Christ, and are given as part of their baptismal experience a new ethical orientation under the guidance of the Holy Spirit" (B4).

72. This perspective emphasizes the awareness that baptism is an ever-present reality to be continually lived out. The baptized are drawn to become more and more "living stones... a chosen race, a royal priesthood, a holy nation, God's own people... [to] proclaim the mighty acts of him who called you out of darkness into his marvellous light" (1 Pet. 2:5,9). These are aspects of life in Christ that Christians share and can witness to together.

73. In their ecumenical efforts to respond to God's call to unity, churches are rediscovering together the ecclesial aspect to this new ethical orientation: baptism is administered by a community of faith that itself lives by God's forgiveness, which is a gift and a calling. Therefore, fundamental to ecumenical effort is the awareness of the relationship between forgiveness and a spirit of conversion, which implies a readiness to confess the sins of one against the other and to be open to the Spirit's gift of *metanoia*. This opens the churches also to the awareness of the need for a healing of memories between them, and to reconciliation. This commitment to *koinonia* flows from the new life in Christ received in baptism and it has Christ himself as pattern. The fifth world conference on Faith and Order reminded us of what koinonia means at both the individual and the collective level and of the relationship of *koinonia* to the very core of the baptismal process of Christian formation (Santiago report, 1993, section I, 20).

74. Recognizing baptism as a bond of unity strengthens the Christian sense of mission and witness and the call to engage together in the common work of the baptized

and believing people of God. Johannes Cardinal Willebrands, then president of the Secretariat for Promoting Christian Unity, wrote about the relation of this bond of unity to mission in 1980:

"By the very fact of baptism each and every Christian is consecrated to the Trinity and called to bear witness to Christ in this baptismal profession of faith in the central Christian truths. There is one baptism and all Christians share, to a greater or lesser extent, a common baptismal profession of faith. This communion based on baptism and the profession of baptismal faith, renders a common witness theologically possible. But since this communion in faith is not complete, such common witness is inevitably limited in its scope.One of the main motives that leads us to seek for unity is the need for all Christians to be able to give a truly and completely common witness to the whole Christian faith" (Cardinal Willebrands, Letter to Episcopal Conference, 22 May 1980, *Information Service*, 43, 1980, II, p.64).

75. Conversion, forgiveness and repentance, such fundamental parts of the biblical heritage, are ethical claims as well. The daily calling to a change of heart and mind *(metanoia)* deepens our faithfulness as Christians. It is a calling to become who we are in Christ. Forgiveness, a gift and a calling, and repentance are signified by the water rite that links the aspect of cleansing and the aspect of life.

76. The last statement opens the perspective that the liturgical life of the church expresses the patterns linking the various aspects of Christian relationship established in baptism: praising God, hearing God's life-giving and prophetic word, participating together with brothers and sisters in the eucharistic meal, interceding for all people in their need, and being sent out to proclaim and to make Christ present in and for the world. The incorporation in Christ, which takes place through baptism, gives rise to a *koinonia* in the church's *kerygma, leiturgia, diakonia and martyria*. These aspects of the church call both for individual and community efforts and witness.

THE CALL TO HOLINESS

77. For all the baptized, growth in Christ implies a call and an empowering to holiness realized by the Spirit: "You shall be holy, for I am holy" (1 Pet. 1:16; cf. also Lev. 11:44, 20:7). BEM reminds us of this universal call to holiness when it says that baptism initiates the reality of a new life given in the midst of the present world, gives participation in the community of the Holy Spirit, and is a sign of the kingdom of God and of the life of the world to come. "Through the gifts of faith, hope and love, baptism has a dynamic which embraces the whole of life, extends to all nations, and anticipates the day when every tongue will confess that Jesus Christ is Lord to the glory of God the Father" (B7).

78. The call to holiness is for all the faithful, and for all it has an eschatological dimension, since all are called to God's kingdom. A distinctive way of living out the vocation to holiness is, in some traditions, constituted by the consecrated life (in monastic or other forms), which is an eschatological sign and also a way of working out the baptismal life, through a particular concern for others and for the whole creation.

ETHICAL FORMATION AS PART OF CONTINUAL GROWTH IN CHRIST

79. From what has already been said, it is clear that ethical formation is part of continual growth in the saving mysteries of Christ. "By baptism, Christians are immersed in the liberating death of Christ where their sins are buried, where the 'old Adam' is crucified with Christ, and where the power of sin is broken" (B3). No longer slaves to sin, but free, the baptized are "fully identified with the death of Christ, they are buried with him and are raised here and now to a new life in the power of the resurrection of Jesus Christ" *(ibid.)*.

80. This ethical orientation springing from baptism should become "intentional" for every baptized person, as a sign of growth in Christ and as a sign of ongoing formation that shapes and models our life-style to Christ's. Such an ethical commitment is an imperative that, along with the missionary imperative, needs to be cultivated and put into practical terms. Thus the churches are required to take responsibility for the formation/education of the faithful. The Joint Working Group itself, in a previous study report concerning "Guidelines for Ecumenical Dialogue on Moral Issues", reminds the churches of the important task of "seeking to be faithful to God in Christ, to be led by the Holy Spirit, and to be a moral environment which helps all members in the formation of Christian conscience and practice". It affirms "the responsibility of every church to provide moral guidance for its members and for society at large" (JWG Seventh Report, p.41).

81. There is, therefore, a deep responsibility for baptized Christians to make their life together, in the words of Pope John Paul II, the building of "the home and the school of communion", a framework in which ethical and moral aspects are part of the building up the *koinonia*:

"A spirituality of communion means, finally, to know how to 'make room' for our brothers and sisters, bearing 'each other's burdens' (Gal. 6:2) and resisting the selfish temptations which constantly beset us and provoke competition, careerism, distrust and jealousy. Let us have no illusions: unless we follow this spiritual path, external structures of communion will serve very little purpose. They would become mechanism without a soul, 'masks' of communion rather than its means of expression and growth" (*Novo Millennio Ineunte*, 2001, 43).

ECCLESIOLOGICAL IMPLICATIONS

82. What has been said in this section suggests several ecclesiological implications. There is general ecumenical agreement that the unity to which Christians are called includes "a common mission witnessing to the gospel of God's grace to all people and serving the whole of creation" (WCC Canberra statement on unity, 1991, 2.1). On the basis of a common baptism separated Christians can, even now, engage in some common witness to the gospel, but still limited in scope because their communion in faith is not yet complete (cf. §68). *An ecclesiological implication of a common baptism is the need for separated Christians to work towards a common understanding of the mission of the church, and to continually resolve divergences in the understanding of faith and morals which prevent them from giving full, common witness to the gospel.*

83. There is also general agreement that the unity to which separated Christians are called is not uniformity, but a *koinonia* characterized by a unity in diversity rooted in a

deep spirituality (cf. Canberra statement, 2.2). Agreement, therefore, that baptism involves a continual, life-long growth in Christ, and a call to holiness (cf. §§77ff.) suggests the following ecclesiological implication: *that in their search for full communion, Christians assess together and find ways of sharing for the benefit of all, those various authentic gifts found in each tradition which foster holiness and life in Christ, and contribute to the church's mission of witnessing to the truth and light of the gospel before the world. In contrast to the mutual isolation that separated Christians have experienced, a sharing of gifts with one another is a way of building up koinonia and, thus, of fostering common witness.*

84. Growth in Christ means growth in holiness, which involves turning away from sin and living the new life of the Spirit. The fact that baptism, as entrance into the church, introduces an individual along this path, or reinforces one who may have begun such a change of life before baptism, draws attention to the following ecclesiological implication. *The Christian community is a moral community of disciples, made up of members who are striving, under the power of God's grace, to live as saints after the pattern of Jesus himself, who called them to be holy as their Father in heaven is holy, and who sent the Holy Spirit to bring this journey to completion. Every Christian community should be a school of prayer and of moral training and personal growth.*

5. Mutual recognition of baptism

85. It is in this perspective that we turn now to the importance of continuing to seek the mutual recognition of baptism as a primary aspect of fostering bonds of unity between separated Christians. "There is one body and one Spirit, just as you were called to the one hope of your calling, one Lord, one faith, one baptism, one God and Father of all, who is above all and through all and in all" (Eph. 4:4-6).

86. Confessing what is in the scriptures, Christians in dialogue have reaffirmed that "we are one people and are called to confess and serve one Lord in each place and in all the world. The union with Christ which we share through baptism has important implications for Christian unity.... Therefore, our one baptism into Christ constitutes a call to the churches to overcome their divisions and visibly manifest their fellowship" (B6).

87. Furthermore, Christians in the ecumenical movement have committed themselves to a long and demanding process of common reflection and action in order to manifest the communion they have rediscovered and recognized through decades of ecumenical dialogue. At the fifth world conference on Faith and Order delegates, in worship, "affirmed and celebrated together the increasing mutual recognition of one another's baptism as the one baptism into Christ". "Indeed such an affirmation has become fundamental for the churches' participation in the ecumenical movement" (cited in *Becoming a Christian*, Faith and Order Paper 184, 1999, §68, p.95).

88. Mutual recognition of baptism is in itself an act of recognition of *koinonia*. It becomes a way in which separated communities manifest the degree of real communion already reached, even if incomplete. There are levels or degrees of mutual recognition reflecting the extent to which separated Christians share the apostolic faith and life. Furthermore, there are different views concerning how much of the apostolic faith needs to be shared prior to mutual recognition and, indeed, in regard to baptism, what constitutes the fullness of the apostolic faith related to it. For example, there would be general

agreement that the apostolic faith is represented when baptism is performed with adequate water in the name of the Father, Son and Holy Spirit. But some would add that to express the apostolic faith completely and faithfully the minister of baptism must be an ordained priest. Others would say that while the minister of baptism must normally be an ordained priest or deacon, in the case of an emergency an "extraordinary" minister can perform a valid baptism. Views held on such issues reflect ecclesiological convictions and might determine for some whether or not mutual recognition of baptism is possible.

THE NEED TO DEFINE TERMS

89. While the conditions allowing mutual recognition increase, there are also problems raised and issues that need further reflection and clarification. Among these is the question of terminology. What is the relationship between recognition and acknowledgment, and the relationship between recognition and reception? Continuing theological reflection and the application of such reflection is urgently needed. Therefore, the JWG is called to survey and seek clarity on these issues. Such an investigation has been already initiated by the Pontifical Council for Promoting Christian Unity through the survey/questionnaire to the episcopal conferences, as well as by Faith and Order through the survey on liturgical rites.

RECOGNITION AND APOSTOLICITY

90. As indicated above, among the issues raised with regard to recognition/reception is the fundamental question of apostolicity. In fact, recognition implies not only a synchronic aspect concerning the relationship among confessions today, but also a diachronic aspect, regarding the relationship with the apostolic heritage handed on over the centuries (cf. Faith and Order consultation on baptism, Faverges, 9).

91. The recognition of the apostolicity of the rite and ordo of baptism is a step towards the full recognition of the apostolicity of the churches in a wider and more profound sense: the full recognition of the same apostolic faith, sacramental order and mission. Full recognition of apostolicity, therefore, involves more than the recognition of baptism. As the world conference on Faith and Order at Santiago de Compostela stated,

"The church seeks to be a community, being faithful as disciples of Christ, living in continuity with the apostolic community established by a baptism inseparable from faith and metanoia, called to a common life in Christ, manifested and sustained by the Lord's supper under the care of a ministry at the same time personal and communal and having as its mission the proclamation in word and witness of the gospel" (Santiago report, p.231).

And as the Decree on Ecumenism stated:

"Baptism therefore constitutes a sacramental bond of unity linking all who have been reborn by means of it. But baptism, of itself, is only a beginning, a point of departure, for it is wholly directed towards the acquiring of fullness of life in Christ. Baptism is thus oriented towards a complete profession of faith, a complete incorporation into the system of salvation such as Christ himself willed it to be, and finally, towards a complete participation in eucharistic communion" (UR, n.22).

Those initiated through baptism continue in an ongoing process of conformity to Christ, both in the dynamics of their individual lives and in those of ecclesial life.

92. In the present stage of the ecumenical movement, separated churches, reflecting unresolved theological issues among them, approach various issues from different ecclesiological perspectives even when there is a common recognition of baptism. An example concerns the relationship of baptism to the eucharist. With regard to the question of what is required for participation in the eucharist, different positions are taken.

93. The churches of the Reformation affirm that the eucharist is a moment of full communion, expressing and enhancing *koinonia*. It is the spiritual basis on which churches live out their baptismal koinonia and express more fully their common confession, worship, witness and service. Furthermore, the churches of the Reformation place primary emphasis on the fact that it is Jesus Christ who invites his disciples to share in the meal. They therefore extend the Lord's hospitality, welcoming to his table all those who love Jesus Christ, have received baptism as a sign of belonging to his body, and have a sufficient understanding of the meaning of the eucharist and its implications. Among many churches of the Reformation the full communion expressed in the eucharist is already experienced in all areas of their faith and life, as reflected in numerous "full communion" or "full mutual recognition" agreements (e.g. Leuenberg and Porvoo). In other cases the full communion expressed in the eucharist is not yet, or incompletely, experienced in all areas of their faith and life. Many such churches have entered into agreements which affirm and celebrate the right of their members, when worshipping in one another's churches, to receive the Lord's hospitality at his table (e.g. the Consultation on Church Union [now Churches Uniting in Christ] in the United States). Such formal, theologically grounded agreements enable these churches to express the baptismal and eucharistic communion which is already theirs in Christ, even as they work to extend this to all areas of their faith and life.

94. The position of the Catholic Church concerning participation in the eucharist takes into account the close relationship of Christ to the church, and of the foundational role of the eucharist in the church. The Second Vatican Council is speaking especially of the eucharist when it describes the liturgy as "the summit towards which the activity of the church is directed; at the same time it is the fount from which all her power flows" (*Sacrosanctum Concilium*, 10). According to the *Directory for the Application of Principles and Norms on Ecumenism* (1993, no. 129), a sacrament is "an act of Christ and of the church through the Spirit" and its celebration in a concrete community is a sign of the reality of its unity in faith, worship and community life. Since sacraments are sources of the unity of the Christian community, of spiritual life, and are the means of building them up, eucharistic communion therefore "is inseparably linked to full ecclesial communion and its visible expression" *(ibid.)*.

At the same time the Catholic Church teaches that by baptism members of other churches and ecclesial communities are brought into a real, even if imperfect, communion with the Catholic Church. Baptism constitutes a sacramental bond of unity among all who through it are reborn, and "is wholly directed towards the acquiring of fullness of life in Christ". The eucharist is for the baptized a spiritual food which enables them to live the life of Christ and to be incorporated more profoundly in him and share more intensely in the mystery of Christ (cf. *ibid.*).

In light of these two basic principles, which must always be taken into account together, the *Directory* states, "that in general the Catholic Church permits access to its eucharistic communion... only those who share its oneness in faith, worship and ecclesial life" *(ibid.)*. For the same reasons, "it also recognizes that in certain circumstances, by way of exception, and under certain conditions", access to the eucharist "may be permitted, or even commended, for Christians of other churches and ecclesial communities" *(ibid.)*. According to the *Directory*, this involves a "grave and pressing need" as usually determined by general norms established by the bishop (no. 130). Among the conditions referred to above is that the person who requests the sacrament "manifest Catholic faith in this sacrament and be properly disposed" (no. 131).

Thus, in this view, mutual recognition of baptism, in itself, is not sufficient for eucharistic communion because the latter is linked to full ecclesial communion in faith and life, and its visible expression.

95. The Orthodox church also places a very strong emphasis on eucharistic sharing as the *final* visible sign of full communion. Such sharing particularly implies confession of one apostolic faith which, though it may be expressed in different *terms*, must necessarily be the same. One of the impediments resides precisely in the necessary verification of this identity in the confession of the same faith. As eucharistic sharing is the expression of full communion, the Orthodox do not practise "eucharistic hospitality" (except in very special cases in which the minister responsible for the eucharist, bishop or priest, pastorally deems it necessary to make an exception; this is an example of *oikonomia*). As far as recognition/reception of baptism is concerned, it must be remembered that in the Orthodox perspective, baptism-chrismation/confirmation-eucharist are one sacrament of initiation.

96. Taking into account these different views of the relationship of baptism to eucharistic sharing, it is important nonetheless that separated Christians give appropriate concrete expression to the common bonds that they share in baptism, so that this relationship is more than one of mere politeness. An important development in recent decades is found in the growing number of invitations to one another to participate in specific, even if limited, ways in major events in each other's churches. For example, the Catholic Church has invited ecumenical partners to participate as fraternal delegates in the assemblies of the synod of bishops in Rome. They are invited to address the assembly and to take part in small group discussions, even though they do not have a vote. It has become normal, too, for other Christian world communions to invite ecumenical partners to their assemblies. On the basis of the common bonds that we share in baptism we have thus begun, though still divided, to enter again into one another's ecclesial life. In order to deepen our relationships, could we not find more such opportunities? Above all, there are many opportunities that can be found for praying for one another, and praying with one another. The annual week of prayer for Christian unity has become an occasion of ecumenical prayer virtually structured into the schedules of all Christian communities, and the opportunities that it offers should not be lost. The week reminds us that prayer for unity is the most important ecumenical activity. It reminds us that our ecumenical journey must be continually supported by prayer throughout the year, and that our ecumenical efforts to pray together are an important way of praising God and begging God's forgiveness for our divisions.

97. From what has just been said, it is clear that even when there is a mutual recognition of baptism, separated churches have different convictions concerning how this relates to other aspects of Christian life. While there are different ecclesiologies at work, there is also the awareness, at the heart of ecumenical dialogue, that each Christian

community, in its life, teaching and practice, has gifts to be discovered and shared. Within the ecumenical movement therefore, churches are constantly called to a "fresh interpretation" of their life, teaching and practice, taking guidance – from this exchange of gifts – for their "worship, educational, ethical and spiritual life and witness" (BEM introduction).

Ecclesiological implications

98. According to the Canberra statement on unity, "the goal of the search for full communion is realized when all the churches are able to recognize in one another the one, holy, catholic and apostolic church in its fullness" (2.1). As seen above, the mutual recognition of baptism implies an acknowledgment of the apostolicity of each other's baptism, but in itself is only a step towards full recognition of the apostolicity of the church involved. *Therefore an ecclesiological implication of the efforts of separated churches to formulate and express mutual recognition of baptism is that when this is accomplished it provides a (or another) substantial basis from which to seek further recognition of apostolicity in one another, and impels those churches towards seeking to express together a shared understanding of the apostolic heritage, of the one, holy, catholic and apostolic church in its fullness.*

6. Ecumenical implications

99. The growing convergence on baptism, and the acknowledgment that through a valid baptism Christians are brought into a real though imperfect communion, has a number of ecumenical implications, suggesting steps that might be taken now to deepen ecumenical relationships. Some of these are the following.

100. (1) Years of dialogue have brought us to the present acknowledgment of a significant convergence on baptism. The churches have the continuing responsibility to foster knowledge of this achievement among their constituencies, and of the fact that this convergence is a major reason why, today, Christians can acknowledge that, though still separated, they share a real though imperfect communion.

101. (2) As stated above (ch. 2, §55) a key affirmation in BEM is that "Baptism is an unrepeatable act. Any practice which might be interpreted as 're-baptism' must be avoided." It is therefore desirable for the churches to seek a common affirmation that it is illegitimate as well as unnecessary to perform baptism to mark rededication to Christ, return to the church after a break in communion, or the reception of special charisms or spiritual gifts. At the same time, reaffirmation and remembrance of one's baptism, in acts that may include elements or "echoes" from the baptismal rite itself, is a proper aspect of Christian worship and spirituality (as when in a baptismal liturgy those present are asked to remember and explicitly affirm their own baptismal confession).

102. (3) Baptism has been a part of the mission and the constitution of the church from earliest times, even before the canon of scripture was established. Recalling this helps us recognize anew the fundamental importance of baptism in the life of the church. The growing ecumenical convergence on baptism has been one of the important achievements of the modern ecumenical movement, and a major factor in fostering new relationships between separated Christians. For these reasons, the importance of baptism in fostering ecumenical reconciliation should be given more visibility in the continuing

ecumenical movement, as an important common factor on which to build. It is recommended therefore that, in the formation of ecumenical instruments or structures which are intended to foster unity among participating churches, such as councils of churches, or similar instruments, reference to baptism should be included in the theological basis of such instruments. In the case of those ecumenical instruments already existing and which do not have baptism as part of their theological basis, on occasions when their constitutions or by-laws are being reviewed, consideration might be given to including baptism as part of the theological basis (cf. ch. 1).

103. (4) In order that the growing convergence on baptism be reflected in local church life, it is recommended that dialogue concerning the significance and valid celebration of baptism take place between authorities of the Catholic Church at the diocesan or episcopal conference level, with the corresponding authorities of WCC member churches in those areas. Thus it should be possible to arrive at common statements through which they express mutual recognition of baptism as well as procedures for considering cases in which doubt may arise as to the validity of a particular baptism (cf. *Directory*, §94). Consideration might be given to developing common baptismal certificates for use by churches in the same region (cf. ch. 1).

104. (5) All Christians who have received the one baptism into Christ's one body have also received a radical calling from God to communion with all the baptized. The growing ecumenical convergence on baptism, with its insights into our shared pattern of baptismal initiation, despite the real variations in practice, offers us new opportunities to act on that calling, and in some ways to undertake common witness together. Out of the conviction that the Holy Spirit draws us towards visible *koinonia*, the churches should seek occasions to express and deepen the existing level of oneness in a common baptism through concrete signs of unity, such as: sending and receiving representatives to be present or take part in each other's baptismal celebrations, praying regularly in our worship for the candidates for baptism and the newly baptized in all the churches, sharing together in aspects of the catechumenate (preparation for baptism) or catechesis (instruction of the newly baptized), reclaiming major Christian festivals such as Easter, Pentecost, Epiphany as common times for the celebration of baptism in our churches.

105. (6) Christians of one communion often still live with bitter memories concerning other Christians, stemming from conflicts of centuries ago which led to divisions which have still not been overcome. These memories are among the primary reasons which make full reconciliation among separated Christians difficult. Since their links to one another in baptism should bring "a wider awareness of the need for healing and reconciliation of memories" (see ch. 4, §73), this should be an impetus to separated Christian communions to take steps towards the healing of memories, as one aspect towards their further reconciliation.

106. (7) One key to ecumenical progress is renewal within each church (cf. *Unitatis Redintegratio* 6). Ecumenical dialogue on baptism implies that consideration be given to internal renewal as well (cf. BEM preface, question 3). The growing ecumenical convergence on baptism should be another reason that proper pastoral practices concerning baptism within each church focus continually on central matters of faith. For example, in those communities in which godparents play a role in baptism, the criteria for choosing godparents for the one to be baptized should relate primarily to the strong faith of the prospective godparent, and not simply to social or family reasons. Not only

would this benefit the one to be baptized, but it would also be an acknowledgment of the close relation between baptism and faith which is one of the basic areas of the emerging ecumenical convergence (cf. ch. 2).

107. (8) All Christians need to give attention to the ongoing communications revolution of today, unprecedented in scope. The mass media can have a forceful and lasting impact on shaping culture, including influencing the way that religious matters are presented to the public. An ecumenical opportunity is offered for Christians to cooperate to the extent possible, and for the sake of the gospel, to see that Christian life and values are presented correctly in the media. The growing convergence on baptism is a reason for Christians to cooperate in presenting to the media information concerning baptism which focuses on the religious dimensions of this sacrament/ordinance. These efforts can help to avoid the creation of a gap between the profound spiritual meaning and significance of baptism as understood by Christians, on the one hand, and impressions of baptism which have appeared in the media, showing baptism as merely a social event, or simply stressing some cultural matters relating to baptism, on the other. Such cooperation would be a way of giving common witness to the gospel.

108. (9) The growing ecumenical convergence on baptism also calls for reflection on other contemporary cultural challenges which, if not faced together by the churches, could have a negative impact on ecumenical relationships. One such challenge is that of inculturation. Some cultures may have a more poetic or doxological way of expressing realities; others use predominately rational forms of expression. In either case, aspects of a particular culture must be brought into the baptismal rite in a way which enhances, rather than diminishes, the normative meaning and symbolism of baptism as rebirth into Christ.

109. (10) Through the ecumenical movement, separated Christians have come to acknowledge a significant degree of *koinonia*. In light of this we ask churches not to allow practices to develop which threaten the unity they now share in respect of the *ordo*, theology and administration of baptism (cf. implication 4, §103 above). One example is the replacement of the traditional Trinitarian baptismal formula (Father, Son, Holy Spirit) with alternative wording. Another example is the admission of persons to the eucharist before baptism (cf. ch. 1 and 2).

110. (11) Churches which share in this growing ecumenical convergence are called to dialogue with churches which are ecumenically engaged, but understand and practise baptism differently, or do not practise it at all. These include (a) churches which baptize "in the name of Jesus" rather than with the traditional Trinitarian formula, but with water; (b) churches which baptize with the traditional Trinitarian formula, but without water; and (c) churches in which entry into the Christian community is effected without baptismal rites. Such dialogue might well focus on the understanding of the Holy Spirit and its role in bringing persons to faith and into the church, and in the believer's lifelong growth into Christ.

Conclusion

111. Baptism is incorporation into the life, death and resurrection of Christ, and therefore is fundamental for Christian life. That it is central for Christian mission is evident from the fact that Our Lord instructed his disciples to "go therefore and make disciples of all nations, baptizing them in the name of the Father and of the Son and of the Holy Spirit..." (Matt. 28:19). As we have explored baptism in this study we have realized more deeply the great gift that baptism is.

112. It is therefore with gratitude to God that we count the growing ecumenical convergence on baptism as one of the important achievements of the modern ecumenical movement. The degree of common understanding of baptism realized thus far has already helped to foster significant new relationships between Christian churches. The *ecumenical implications* listed just above, in part six of this study document, are intended to suggest ways in which the convergences achieved on baptism can be consolidated and received into the life of the churches so that further steps forward towards unity can be built on solid foundations. The *ecclesiological implications* mentioned in each of the other sections indicate that the convergences on baptism relate to other issues to which attention must be given in continuing dialogue if further steps towards visible unity are to be taken.

113. It is hoped that this study document, by illustrating the extent of mutual agreement on baptism discovered thus far, will enable Christians to respond together, to the extent possible now, to the Lord's commission to "go therefore and make disciples of all nations...," and to invite those who have not heard the gospel before to life in Christ through baptism.

A NOTE ON PROCESS:

Initial material presented for reflection to the JWG executive in January 2000 included a summary of implications of baptism derived from many responses to BEM (John Radano) and an overview of current Faith and Order work on baptism (Alan Falconer). The two were asked to coordinate the project. After the JWG plenary in May 2000 developed five main areas which became the focus of discussion for the study, drafting meetings took place in 2001 and 2002 (Geneva), February 2003 (Rome), and September 2003 (Geneva). Work in progress on the study was presented each year for discussion at annual JWG meetings. Participating in drafting sessions were Eugene Brand (2001, 2002), Thomas Best (2001, 2002, September 2003), Gosbert Byamungu (2001), Alan Falconer (2001, 2002, September 2003), Mark Heim (2001, 2002, February 2003), Nicholas Lossky (February 2003), Thomas Pott, osb (2002, February 2003), John Radano (2001, 2002, February and September 2003), Teresa Francesca Rossi (2002, February 2003), Liam Walsh op (2002, February 2003). Drafting was also done through correspondence between February and September 2003 by Heim, Lossky, Radano, Rossi, Walsh. Teresa Rossi did additional research on media presentations on baptism for the project, and William Henn contributed suggestions for improving certain aspects of an advanced draft of the text. David Hamid reviewed the advanced text for editorial clarity and consistency. The study document was approved at the JWG plenary meeting in Crete, in May 2004.

NOTES

¹ In one dialogue report, Pentecostals said that they "do not see the unity between Christians as being based in a common water baptism, mainly because they believe that the New Testament does not base it on baptism. Instead the foundation of unity is a common faith and experience of Jesus Christ as Lord and Saviour through the Holy Spirit" (*Perspectives on Koinonia*, report of the third phase of the international Pentecostal-Catholic dialogue, 1990 §55). Concerning Evangelicals see for example "The Evangelical-Roman Catholic Dialogue on Mission, 1977-1984", in *Growth in Agreement II*, p. 422.

² The most recent ecumenical description of the unity that is being sought is the Canberra statement, "The Unity of the Church As Koinonia: Gift and Calling", approved by the World Council of Churches assembly at Canberra, Australia, 1991. This will be referred to at several points.

The Nature and Purpose of Ecumenical Dialogue

A JWG Study

Introduction

DIALOGUE: A GIFT TO THE CHURCHES

1. Since the establishment of the contemporary ecumenical movement in the 20th century a "culture of dialogue" has emerged. Throughout the first half of the century, the philosophical, cultural and theological presuppositions for such a culture were elaborated. Such a culture has led to new relationships between communities and societies. However there has also emerged a counter–culture, fuelled by fundamentalism, new experiences of vulnerability, new political realities such as the ending of the cold war and the bringing into relationship peoples with very different visions and goals, and the impact of globalization which has led to increased awareness of ethnic and national identities. This has been manifested further in the destabilization of institutions and value systems and a questioning of authority. Dialogue has become a *sine qua non* for nations churches and cultures. For the Christian churches, dialogue is an imperative arising from the gospel, which thus presents a counter-challenge to those who would adopt exclusivist positions.

2. This document charts the impact of the culture of dialogue on the churches, offers a theological reflection on the nature of dialogue, and suggests a spirituality which can guide Christians and their communities in their approach to one another. It is an attempt on the basis of experience gained since 1967 to encourage the churches to continue their ecumenical dialogue with commitment and perseverance.

3. The Joint Working Group between the Roman Catholic Church and the World Council of Churches was formed in 1965. It began its work by reflecting on the nature of dialogue. In 1967, it published a report entitled "Ecumenical Dialogue", which has served since then as a useful reference. The experience of the multilateral dialogues of Faith and Order since 1927 and of church union negotiations, such as those in South India, provided insights for the Joint Working Group as it undertook its task.

The year 1967 did not mark the beginning of ecumenical dialogues, but due to the active participation of the Roman Catholic Church after the Second Vatican Council, ecumenical dialogues received a new energy and scope. They soon developed into a key instrument for ecumenical progress.

4. Almost forty years have passed. The Joint Working Group again presents a study document on "The Nature and Purpose of Ecumenical Dialogue". Organized dialogues have taken place at local, national and international levels involving all major churches and confessional communions. Substantial achievements have been reached and the participating bodies have clarified positions, and consensus has emerged on important matters of division and remaining obstacles to unity have been identified. In the meantime, the context of dialogue has changed, the reflection on dialogue has continued and the urgency of seeking visible unity through honest and persistent dialogue seeking truth with love has increased.

5. Since 1967 relations between different churches, Christian world communions and Christian families have grown and developed as a result of dialogue. Dialogue has encouraged churches to understand one other, and has helped to shatter stereotypes, break down historic barriers and encourage new and more positive relationships. Some examples include:

- the 1965 common declaration of Pope Paul VI and the Ecumenical Patriarch Athenagoras I which removed from the memory and midst of the church the sentences of excommunication mutually pronounced in 1054;

- the Christological agreement between the Roman Catholic Church and the Assyrian Church of the East (1994);

- the Joint Declaration on the Doctrine of Justification signed by the Lutheran World Federation and the Catholic Church in 1999, which states that the condemnations of each other's view of justification pronounced during the Reformation period in the Lutheran confessions and the Council of Trent do not apply today, insofar as they hold the understanding of that doctrine found in the Joint Declaration.

These are significant stages on the path towards mutual recognition, communion and the visible unity of the church.

6. The results of international dialogues have fostered a number of new church relationships. The Faith and Order statement, *Baptism, Eucharist and Ministry* (BEM 1982), and bilateral dialogues combined to lay the foundations for the Meissen, Porvoo, and "Called to Common Mission" agreements between Anglicans and Lutherans in different parts of the world. The bilateral agreement between Orthodox and Oriental Orthodox churches has facilitated reconciliation between these church families. The theological dialogue of the Anglican–Roman Catholic International Commission (ARCIC) has led to the establishment of a new commission to foster growth in communion between these churches, through the reception of the agreements and the development of strategies for strengthening the fellowship (Iarccum – International Anglican-Roman Catholic Commission for Unity and Mission).

7. Dialogues have also helped to challenge and change attitudes in communities living in tense situations.

8. Insights from the dialogues have led different churches towards renewal and change in their life, teaching and patterns of worship. For example, BEM has encouraged more frequent celebrations of the sacrament of the Lord's supper in some communities, and influenced revision of their liturgy itself.

9. Since 1967 it is clear that a culture of dialogue has emerged among some churches which influences every aspect of Christian living. It is evident in projects of collaboration as members of different communities seek to address the needs of those who are marginalized in our world. It is also seen in a variety of discussion groups involving members of different communities. It is an attitude of openness to other communities and their members.

10. His Holiness Pope John Paul II has called this culture "the dialogue of conversion" where, together, Christians and communities seek forgiveness for sins against unity and live into the space where Christ, the source of the church's unity, can effectively act, with all the power of the Spirit (*Ut Unum Sint*, 34, 35). While the attitude of dialogue is to be evident in every aspect of Christian living, engagement in international and bilateral dialogues is a very specific form of dialogue.

TWO APPROACHES TO DIALOGUE

11. Since 1967 two distinct approaches to this specific form of ecumenical dialogue have been evident, each with its own character and each addressing different, but related, aspects of the quest for full communion.

12. The bilateral dialogues between officially appointed representatives of two Christian world communions or church families seek to overcome historical difficulties between these communities. Attention is paid to the history and classic texts which define those communities, and to the current issues, past and present, which have inhibited relations between them and which hinder movement towards communion. These dialogues normally identify that which is held in common, clarify differences, seek solutions and encourage collaboration where possible.

13. The multilateral dialogues operate in a wider framework, with officially appointed representatives of churches seeking to draw on the wisdom of all Christian traditions to investigate a theological issue. This has enabled distinctions to be made on issues over which Christians have been divided (e.g. between *episkope* and episcopacy), offering bilateral dialogues new approaches to historical difficulties. Christians have been reminded that multilateral and bilateral dialogue takes place within the context of the mission of the church and as such are in the service of the unity of the church "so that the world might believe…" (John 17:21). Multilateral dialogue has also emphasized that non-doctrinal factors are important for understanding doctrinal divisions; such divisions have occurred for a multiplicity of reasons – political, cultural, social, economic, and racial as well as doctrinal – and these factors also need to be addressed in processes of reconciling and healing memories.

14. Both multilateral and bilateral dialogues are essential for the dialogical process. At best there is a continuing interaction between them, with each drawing on insights gained in the other. All dialogue will be subject to the historical and cultural context which influences the relations between different communities.

NEW CONTEXT OF DIALOGUE

15. While churches have embraced a culture of dialogue and it is possible to chart a number of achievements arising from the engagement in formal ecumenical conversations, new factors have emerged in the thirty-six years since the publication of "Ecumenical Dialogue" which signify a new context in which such dialogue takes place.

16. While dialogue has led to increased sensitivity and ecumenical commitment among ecclesial traditions, a renewed allegiance to confessional identity has also developed, leading possibly to exclusivist confessionalism. There has often been a reluctance to change in the light of the results of dialogue. Sometimes this has been caused by the difficulty of achieving wider consensus within the different churches. Difficulties in reception have sometimes led to division *within* confessions, since it is increasingly clear that no church or confessional tradition is a homogeneous entity. In some cases, reception has been made more difficult as divisions within and between some churches have emerged on cultural and ethical issues – matters rarely the subject of the dialogues themselves. For some churches the issues being addressed in the international bilateral and multilateral dialogues are perceived as remote from their existential concerns. After over thirty years of theological dialogue and despite significant agreements during this period, not all issues required to lead to unity between churches have been resolved. The process of reconciliation has been slow. For some, and for different reasons, this has put in question the value of undertaking such theological dialogues.

17. Yet it is clear in every part of the world that the gospel of reconciliation cannot be proclaimed credibly by churches which are themselves not reconciled with each other. Divided churches are a counter-witness to the gospel.

18. What can be learned from the experience of dialogue about the nature of ecumenical dialogue itself? The new context suggests that a re-examination of ecumenical dialogue is needed, lifting up the insights of "Ecumenical Dialogue" from 1967, reflecting on over three decades of multilateral and bilateral dialogue activity, and considering challenges which have arisen.

The nature and purpose of ecumenical dialogue

TOWARDS A DESCRIPTION OF ECUMENICAL DIALOGUE

19. Ecumenical dialogue is pursued in response to Our Lord's prayer for his disciples "that they may all be one so that the world may believe" (John 17:21). It is essentially a conversation, a speaking and a listening between partners. Each speaks from his or her context and ecclesial perspective. Dialogic speech seeks to communicate that experience and perspective to the other, and to receive the same from the other in order to enter into their experience and see the world through the other's eyes, as it were. The aim of dialogue is that each understands the partner in a deep way. It is a spiritual experience in understanding the other, a listening and speaking to one another in love.

20. Dialogue entails walking with the other; pilgrimage is an apt metaphor for dialogue. Dialogue represents a word – neither the first nor the last – on a common journey, marking a moment between the "already" of our past histories and the "not yet" of our future. It images the disciples' conversation on the road to Emmaus, recounting the wonders the Lord has worked during a journey culminating in the recognition of the Lord in the breaking of bread at a common table.

21. Dialogue is more than an exchange of ideas. It is a "mutual gift exchange". It is a process through which together we seek to transcend divisions by clarification of past misunderstandings through historical studies, or bypass obstacles by discovering new language or categories. And more: it involves being receptive to the ethos of the

other, and those aspects of Christian tradition preserved in the heritage of the other. Different church traditions have often given preference to certain biblical texts and traditions over others. In the process of dialogue, we are invited to reappropriate these and thus witness to the richness of the gospel in its integrity.

22. An important focus of dialogue involves mutual exploration of the meaning of the apostolic faith. At the same time dialogues are conducted within the context of the living faith of communities in particular times and places; thus they should always reflect contextual experience. They do not simply focus on systems or formulae of belief but on how these are lived out by the communities involved in the dialogue. This is particularly true with regard to national dialogues. While context is also an essential consideration in international dialogue, in this case, no particular local context can dominate, and the total, often complex, self-understanding of a Christian world communion is taken into consideration.

23. Furthermore, there is another difference in regard to context. It stems from the very different understandings found among the Christian world communions concerning the relationship between the local and universal expressions of the church. This in turn has an influence on the impact of contextual experience within the whole. Thus, for many, final authority (and therefore an aspect of independence to one degree or another) rests in each member church of a world communion (e.g., in churches stemming from the Reformation). In another case (e.g. the Catholic Church), bonds of communion of a theological, canonical and spiritual nature govern the relationships between the particular churches and the universal church. The very understanding of a particular or local church involves its being in communion with every other local church and with the church of Rome. Thus there is a continual mutual influence between the particular and universal expressions of the church. While particular and universal expressions of the church are interdependent, priority is given to the unity of the whole.

24. Dialogue addresses the divisions of the past, examining them through scholarship, seeking to state what the dialogue partners can say together about the faith today. Dialogue seeks to discern the evangelical character of the present faith, life, and worship of the partner. Thus dialogue has a descriptive character.

THEOLOGICAL FOUNDATIONS OF DIALOGUE

25. Ecumenical dialogue reflects analogically the inner life of the Triune God and the revelation of his love. The Father communicates himself through his Word, his Son who, in turn, responds to the Father in the power of the Spirit – a communion of life. In the fullness of time, God spoke to us through his Son (cf. Heb 1: 1-2); God's Word became flesh and dwelt among us (John 1:14).

26. The exchange between the Father and the Son in the power of the Spirit establishes the mutual interdependence of the three persons of the Triune God. In God's self–communication to God's people, God invites us to receive his word and respond in love. Thus we enter through a participation in God's gracious activity and the imperative of Christian obedience into communion with God who is communion – Father, Son and Holy Spirit. In emulating this dialogical pattern of speaking and listening, of revealing ourselves and receiving the other, we leave our illusion of self-sufficiency and isolation and enter a relationship of communion.

27. The very nature of human existence also emphasizes that we do not live or exist without each other. "We not only have encounter, we are encounter. The other is not the limit of myself; the other is part of and an enrichment of my own existence. Dialogue thus belongs to the reality of human existence. Identity is dialogical" (H.E. Cardinal Kasper).

Presuppositions of dialogue

28. Ecumenical dialogue presupposes our common incorporation in Christ, through faith and baptism and the action of the Holy Spirit and we recognize in one another faith communities seeking oneness in Christ (see the JWG statement, "Ecclesiological and Ecumenical Implications of a Common Baptism", 2004). Within ecumenical dialogue we meet not as strangers but as co-dwellers within the household of God, as Christians who through our communion with the Triune God already experience "a real, though imperfect communion" (*Unitatis Redintegratio*, 3).

29. Thus ecumenical dialogue presupposes engagement in prayer. It assumes a cruciform pattern, at the intersection of our "vertical" relationship with God and our "horizontal" communion with one another. In this we also imitate Christ's self-giving and vulnerability. We turn from our self-absorption and self-interests to the experience of the other, assuming the vulnerability of allowing ourselves to be known by the other and of allowing ourselves to see another's Christian pattern of life, witness, and worship through their eyes. Within this reciprocal exchange we allow ourselves to experience a fusion of horizons, enabling us to heal our divisions, strengthen our common witness, and engage in the shared mission of furthering God's reign.

The purpose of ecumenical dialogue

30. The goal of ecumenical dialogue as expressed in the Canberra statement "The Unity of the Church as Koinonia: Gift and Calling" is that of the ecumenical movement itself:

"The unity of the church to which we are called is a *koinonia* given and expressed in the common confession of the apostolic faith; a common sacramental life entered by the one baptism and celebrated together in one eucharistic fellowship; a common life in which members and ministries are mutually recognized and reconciled; and a common mission witnessing to the gospel of God's grace to all people and serving the whole of creation. The goal of the search for full communion is realized when all the churches are able to recognize in one another the one, holy, catholic and apostolic church in its fullness. This full communion will be expressed on the local and the universal levels through conciliar forms of life and action. In such communion churches are bound in all aspects of their life together at all levels in confessing the one faith and engaging in worship and witness, deliberation and action" (2.1).

31. Dialogue aims not only at agreement on doctrine, but also at the healing of memories through repentance and mutual forgiveness. It may also be an avenue for exploring those activities we can pursue together, in order to undertake together everything that we are not obliged to do separately, as was expressed in the statement of the Faith and Order conference at Lund in 1952.

32. Christian unity is a gift of the Holy Spirit, not a human achievement. Dialogue prepares for that gift, prays for it, and celebrates it once received.

33. Ecumenical dialogue is ecclesial; the participants come as representatives of their ecclesial traditions, seeking to represent their tradition while exploring the divine mysteries with representatives of other traditions (cf. *Directory for the Application of Principles and Norms on Ecumenism*, 176).

34. Dialogue assumes an equality of the participants, as partners working together for Christian unity. It exhibits reciprocity, so that partners are not expected to adopt "our" structures for dialogue (cf. *Ut Unum Sint*, 27).

35. As dialogue proceeds, it is important to be conscious of the "hierarchy of truths" where not everything is presented at the same level of integration with the essential doctrines of the Christian faith (cf. *Directory, supra*, 176).

36. Doctrinal formulations of the faith are culturally and historically conditioned. One and the same faith can be expressed in different language at different times, reflecting new insights and organic developments. The awareness of this has proved to be a liberating experience in dialogues and has helped to create possibilities for the development of new understandings and relationships. The process of discerning a consensus in faith, must take into account different approaches, emphases, and language respecting the diversity and the limits to diversity within and among the dialogue partners.

The spirituality and practice of ecumenical dialogue

SPIRITUALITY

37. Since Christian life is itself dialogical (cf. §§23-24 *supra*) ecumenical dialogue is a way of being, of living the Christian life. Although it has specific features, it presupposes a broad spirituality of openness to the other in light of the imperative of Christian unity, directed by the Holy Spirit. Dialogue is a process of discernment, and as such requires patience, since ecumenical progress may be slow. Humility is required in order to be open to receiving truth from another. Commitment in love is also required, to search together to manifest that unity willed by our Lord. Thus we may include the following considerations about a spirituality for dialogue.

SPIRITUALITY FOR DIALOGUE PARTNERS AS COMMUNITIES

38. Communities engaging in dialogue commit themselves to a shared journey. While conducted by just a few persons on each side, a dialogue aims to assist those communions involved to move step by step towards unity by working to ensure that each partner understands, to the degree possible how the life and witness of the other can be beneficial for all. When this aspect of dialogue is neglected, dialogue results will seem remote from the experience of the church and may not be received into its life and transform relationships. Furthermore, when this aspect of dialogue is neglected, the ecumenical endeavour itself becomes an excuse for maintaining the status *quo ante*. Thus ecumenical dialogue implies new spiritual obligations not only for individual participants, but also for the communities as a whole.

39. A willingness to change through dialogue requires seeing the other differently, changing our patterns of thinking, speaking and acting towards the other. Since Christian unity is realized through God's power, not our own, dialogue is also a process of conversion, of discernment, of being attentive to God's impulse. It opens us up for judgment and renewal. Thus in seeking openness to transformed and reconciled relationships, we explore processes of healing and forgiveness.

40. Dialogue with Christians from whom we are divided requires examining how our identity has been constructed in opposition to the other, i.e. how we have identified ourselves by what we are not. To overcome polemical constructions of identity requires new efforts to articulate identity in more positive ways, distinguishing between confessional identity as a sign of fidelity to faith, and confessionalism as an ideology constructed in enmity to the other. This entails a spiritual as well as a theological preparation for ecumenical dialogue. Through understanding mutual hurts and expressing and receiving forgiveness we move from fear of one another to bearing one another's burdens, to being called to suffer together. Commitment to dialogue requires, at the least, a review of how our church educates its members about the dialogue partner(s).

41. Preparation for dialogue includes recovering theological resources for the development and refinement of doctrine within our *own* tradition. This requires a willingness to be challenged by, and to learn from, others. As encounter deepens, we find ourselves incorporating theological reflection from the partner's tradition(s) into our own life, embracing the other's thoughts and words as our own.

42. Our common commitment to Christian unity requires not only prayers for one another but a life of common prayer.

Practice

43. Each dialogue is unique and must take into account the factors drawing these partners into this dialogue at this time. Here the following points may be relevant.

CONFIGURATIONS OF DIALOGUE PARTNERS

44. The configuration of partners will necessarily affect the practice of each dialogue. To agree the goals and methods for the dialogue, whether bilateral or multilateral, it is critical to understanding who the partners are, the origin of their divisions, and/or the way these Christian communities have related to each other in the past.

45. Each partner has a particular understanding of the history of the divisions. One or both may have neuralgic memories of power and victimisation stemming from the actions of representatives of the other community in dialogue. There may be considerable asymmetries between partners (e.g. of size, ecclesial self-understanding, ability to speak on behalf of the larger ecclesial community, majority or minority status). Dialogue must consider such asymmetries, with each partner understanding the other's entry point. Many dialogue partners are also engaged in other dialogues, both bilateral and multilateral. Dialogues should be interrelated, and influence one another.

46. Dialogue aiming at Christian unity demands more than cooperation on non-divisive matters. We bring to ecumenical dialogue all that falls outside the Lund principle which asks: "whether they [churches] should not act together in all matters except those in which deep differences of conviction compel them to act separately". Where conscience has, thus far, forbidden unity, we engage in dialogue precisely to clarify and overcome these past and present deep differences of conviction.

47. The subjects for dialogue are drawn from the partners' past and present relationship. In discerning topics to pursue we might ask: "Where, in our relationship as dialogue partners, is the gospel at stake? What prevents us from fully recognizing one another?" Context will influence the choice of dialogue topics; yet these topics will be all the more relevant if understood within the wider spectrum of the basic, historic Christian divisions.

48. The choice of topics should be informed by history. Although each generation must reappropriate what has come before, we should not forget that we are contributing to a journey which began before us and will continue after us.

49. Topics may include not only formulations of doctrine, but also ways of doing theology and using sources of faith. Methodologies may themselves become the subject of dialogue. Choosing points of departure requires discernment of what is ripe for discussion. It may be important to begin by examining what *unites* the partners; the most divisive questions may need to be set aside until a shared experience of trust makes it possible to tackle them. But dialogue between divided churches cannot postpone indefinitely an examination of the issues at the crux of their division.

50. Dialogues that have matured through considerable agreement on areas of conflict may be drawn on to further constructive engagement on particular issues.

Methodologies

DIVERSE CONTEXTS AND APPROACHES

51. Since different dialogue topics call for different methodologies, we cannot speak of *one* way of approaching dialogue. Each partner will be more comfortable with some methods than others. We should not assume that certain ways of engaging one another should be favoured over others.

52. The experience of ecumenical dialogue in the 20th century has shown how important it is to examine the historical and socio-economic factors affecting doctrinal issues. Situating doctrinal formulations in their historical context can free us to express the same faith in new ways today. This methodology that resulted in the Joint Declaration on the Doctrine of Justification modelled a hermeneutic which may be fruitful elsewhere.

53. The work on hermeneutics by the Faith and Order commission (*A Treasure in Earthen Vessels*, Faith and Order Paper 182, 1998) draws attention to how we "read" our own story as a community, and how we find points of convergence with the stories of others. A "hermeneutics of coherence" suggests sympathetic awareness of the faith and witness of others, as complementary to our own. A "hermeneutics of confidence" suggests that mutual reception and recognition is possible through the Holy Spirit's gifts to

the Christian community. A "hermeneutics of suspicion" suggests the question, "Whose interests are being served by this particular reading?" Because dialogue serves the cause of the one gospel of Jesus Christ, each mode of "reading" can lead us together into greater understanding of the truth.

54. Dialogue is not negotiation towards a "lowest common denominator", but a search for new entry-points in order to discover the way forward together. Sometimes dialogues confront issues which gave rise to mutual condemnations in the past. Here it can help to clarify what the actual position of each side was at that time and how each sought, through their position, to preserve the integrity of the gospel in a particular context. Perhaps the demands of the gospel *today* enable the partners to find common ground.

55. Not all doctrinal conflicts can be easily resolved. Therefore a careful consideration of the positions – how far they are complementary, and where and how they diverge – can be very useful in furthering the churches' growth in ecumenical relationships.

PARTICIPANTS AND COMPETENCIES

56. A variety of competencies are required in ecumenical dialogue today. Those with historical and doctrinal expertise are necessary; but so are those bringing other forms of expertise, such as liturgists, ethicists, missiologists, and those with pastoral oversight responsibilities. The broader a church's participation in a dialogue, the more applicable will be its findings for the life of the church as a whole. Different churches have different understandings of how an individual "represents" the church in a dialogue, but all participants should be aware that they stand within the discipline of their tradition and are accountable to it.

57. As "Ecumenical Dialogue" advises. it is often appropriate to include observers in the dialogue, to recognize and encourage the wider ecumenical implications of the work.

The reception of ecumenical dialogues

58. If the agreements reached through ecumenical dialogue are to have an impact on the life and witness of the churches and lead to a new stage of communion, then careful attention needs to be paid to processes for receiving the agreements so that the whole community might be involved in the process of discernment.

THE MEANING OF RECEPTION

59. "Reception" is the process by which the churches make their own the results of all their encounters with one other, and in a particular way the convergences and agreements reached on issues over which they have historically been divided. As the report of the sixth forum on bilateral dialogues notes:

"Reception is an integral part of the movement towards that full communion which is realized when "all the churches are able to recognise in one another the one, holy, catholic and apostolic church in its fullness" [Canberra statement].

Thus reception is far more than the official responses to the dialogue results, although official responses are essential. However, even though they are not concerned with the full range of interchurch relations, the results of international theological dialogues are a crucial aspect of reception, as specific attempts to overcome what divides churches and impedes the expression of unity willed by our Lord.

INSTRUMENTS OF RECEPTION

60. Churches have developed appropriate modes and instruments for receiving the results of bilateral and multilateral international dialogues. The structures and processes of decision-making that determine the "mind" of a church or community of churches reflect each church or communion's self-understanding and polity and their particular approach.

DIFFICULTIES IN RECEPTION

61. Churches have encountered difficulties in the process of reception in part because of different modes and processes of reception.

62. Issues of consistency have emerged. When a church community is involved in several dialogues with partners from different ecclesial traditions, the presentation of its self-understanding must be consistent with what is said to all the partners, and the results achieved in one dialogue must be coherent with those achieved in the others. Some Christian world communions (the Anglican communion, the World Alliance of Reformed churches, the Lutheran World Federation) have developed structures to test this.

63. Issues of perceived relevance have emerged. Are the subjects of ecumenical dialogue largely those on the agenda of European and North American churches, even if the doctrinal divisions in question were transported throughout the world through missionary activity?

64. How do international dialogues relate to pastoral and theological priorities of the local churches? If the issues addressed are not existential questions faced by the churches, reception becomes difficult. New ways are needed to help churches see that disunity contradicts the gospel of reconciliation. How can the results of international dialogues engage the churches existentially in their different contexts? Many factors inhibiting the reception of dialogues are non-doctrinal. Where majority and minority tensions are evident, processes of forgiveness, healing and reconciliation must proceed before, and alongside, processes of reception.

65. By their very nature, dialogues are conducted by officially appointed representatives, competent in the issues under discussion. But reception, while a process of discernment by the leadership of the churches, also involves the discernment of the whole people of God. Insensitivity to the need for education and discernment by the *whole* community has made reception difficult. "Top-down" rather than "bottom-up" language has appeared at critical points in some processes. Thus while dialogues seek communion among churches, they may lead to the formation of dissenting groups and divisions *within* churches.

POSITIVE EXPERIENCES IN RECEPTION

66. How might reception processes be conducted so as to overcome these problems? In the past thirty years several international dialogues have been widely received, leading to new expressions of church fellowship and the renewal of the churches

involved. Perhaps these can provide some clues about what is essential if reception is to take place.

A MULTILATERAL CASE STUDY

67. The multilateral dialogue leading to *Baptism, Eucharist and Ministry* offers one such example. The BEM process required time, constant dialogue with the churches, the provision of study materials, serious consideration of responses to the draft texts, translations into many languages, building upon what had been previously achieved in dialogue, and drawing on other dialogues and ecumenical initiatives.

68. This process took nearly twenty years, and indeed there had been discussion of the issues for a prior forty years. In the period 1963-82 the draft-in-process was sent three times to churches, theological colleges and ecumenical instruments for comment and reaction. The drafts were published widely, and comments taken seriously in each stage of redrafting. Many churches encouraged discussions of drafts in congregations, thus involving the whole community. Drafters also drew on international bilateral dialogues on related subjects, and on insights from the liturgical movement. The multilateral approach went behind the divisions between the churches, seeking biblical roots for understanding the specific issues (e.g. *anamnesis*). This provided points of reference, placing historical differences in a fresh perspective.

69. Whenever it became clear that agreement on a particular issue was going to be elusive, the specific issue was addressed by a gathering of theologians (e.g. the relation between baptism of those making a personal profession of faith and infant baptism; the issue of episcopacy). From these consultations new language was found enabling agreement to be expressed.

70. Once finalized and acclaimed by the Faith and Order commission in 1982, the text was sent to the churches for response. Carefully crafted questions accompanied the document, so that the churches in a process of discernment could receive it. An accompanying commentary facilitated understanding by those not party to the discussion. A volume of theological essays encouraged discussion in theological colleges, while a collection of liturgical materials assisted churches in reflecting on the relation between their theological understanding and liturgical practice. To give a liturgical expression to the eucharistic agreement, a liturgy was developed which illustrated what the convergence enabled in respect of celebrating the sacrament. This "Lima liturgy" undoubtedly helped to popularize the BEM agreement and process.

71. BEM was translated into more than thirty languages, facilitating its reception around the world. The process was enhanced by seminars led by Faith and Order commissioners and staff. Study guides were produced in various contexts, assisting congregational and interchurch discussions of the text. The process which from the beginning engaged the churches in the actual development of the text, facilitated official responses "at the highest level of authority" when the text was completed in 1982. Some 186 responses were received and published in six volumes. This resulted in the text having an unprecedented ecumenical authority, which in turn encouraged churches to develop new relationships with each other.

72. On the basis of this convergence several churches were able to enter new relationships of communion (e.g. Lutheran and Anglican churches in Nordic and Baltic countries, Britain, Ireland, Canada, Germany, United States; Reformed and Lutherans

in the United States; United/Uniting churches in South Africa…). Other churches were encouraged, through responding to the questions, to renew the frequency and liturgical content of their eucharistic celebrations. The distinctions made concerning ministry have facilitated bilateral dialogues, even in situations where these issues had become difficult to pursue.

SOME BILATERAL CASE STUDIES

73. Several international bilateral dialogues also developed mechanisms and work patterns which have fostered reception.

74. The official signing of the Joint Declaration on the Doctrine of Justification was the result of a series of events of Lutheran-Catholic cooperation. The Joint Declaration drew from results of more than thirty years of international and national dialogue. In 1991, having decided to focus more on the reception of dialogue results, the Lutheran World Federation and the Pontifical Council for Promoting Christian Unity developed a working paper entitled "Strategies for Reception: Perspectives on the Reception of Documents Emerging from the Lutheran-Catholic International Dialogue". In 1993, they established a small joint commission to draft a Joint Declaration on the Doctrine of Justification. Each side then submitted the draft to its respective internal processes of evaluation. The results of the evaluation led to a revision of the draft. At every stage each side was supported by the highest levels of authority. The final version of the joint declaration was formally accepted by both sides in 1998 and signed in 1999. The successful reception of the declaration was helped by the close collaboration between the two partners in the reception process.

75. The agreement resulting from the dialogue between Reformed churches and Mennonite churches was sealed through a visit to the battle sites at which their forces had fought in the Reformation period. The churches repented, received forgiveness for allowing the memory of these events to determine present-day relationships, and sought to initiate a new relationship. A constant interplay of agreement, comment and elucidation by the bodies sponsoring the Anglican-Roman Catholic International Commission may have facilitated the reception of its dialogue reports. A concern in several dialogues involving the World Alliance of Reformed churches and the Roman Catholic Church was relating the theological agenda to actual Reformed-Roman Catholic relations around the world. This was an early attempt to hold together the agendas of a dialogue and of local churches.

SOME CONCLUSIONS CONCERNING RECEPTION

76. Since 1967 several factors essential to reception processes can be discerned. For dialogue results to be appropriated, the widest possible engagement with the community and their theologians is needed. This is best effected by interchange at appropriate points in the development of a text between persons engaged in dialogues and the churches concerned, with the text being developed in light of comments received.

77. The process is enhanced by sharing biblical, theological, and liturgical resources which help communities understand the journey undertaken by the drafters and situate the theme both within the confessions involved and within contemporary scholarship. The text should be translated into all appropriate languages, and accompa-

nied by study guides (written by members of the drafting group, since only they know the road travelled to reach agreement). Reception can be enhanced by appropriate symbolic gestures by the sponsoring bodies, indicating that a new stage on the journey towards fuller manifestation of communion has been reached.

78. For reception and for subsequent implementation it is important to devise instruments for cooperative oversight. In the light of agreements reached, consideration needs to be given to processes of reception which involve both communities seeking to discern together. At present many reception processes are conducted within each community separately.

79. Visits between communities foster growth in relationship. It should become natural to invite partners to significant events in the life of the church, and to encourage Christian friendships at the local level. The ecumenical movement includes a spirituality of hospitality, of willingness to receive the other in our own place. Commitment to dialogue requires the willingness of church leaders to be examples of new openness, for example through shared symbolic acts, visits, and being present in times of joy and sorrow. All of these contacts foster mutual understanding and the reception of dialogue results.

Challenges for dialogue in the 21st century

80. The ecumenical movement has helped Christians move from the churches' virtual isolation from one another, experienced for centuries due to 5th-, 11th-, or 16th-century divisions. By the end of the 20th century, the churches could speak of a new relationship of sharing even now a "real, though imperfect", communion. Given these achievements, what are the challenges for ecumenical dialogue in the 21st century?

81. While these achievements have been considerable, during this same period there has also been a tendency to greater fragmentation and fracture between and within churches. There are those who assert strongly that dialogue is inimical to the Christian tradition, and who wish to assert claims of absoluteness and uniqueness. Under the influence of post-modern culture authority structures and authority in all aspects of life have been called into question. This raises challenges within the churches to doctrinal statements and to structures of governance as well. Some question whether it is at all possible for any one of any group to represent a community. The treatment of ethical questions in revolutionary ways by society has increasingly influenced the way these issues appear on the agenda of the churches, where it is clear that different views and approaches are discussed across denominational and confessional lines. It is crucial that these features of contemporary church life are taken into account as the culture of dialogue is developed in this decade.

82. However, we limit ourselves to some broader perspectives which must be considered, and to some challenges to the ecumenical movement and to dialogue in particular.

THE CHALLENGE OF A CHANGING WORLD

83. The broad context in which people live today, characterized by an increasingly interdependent and inter-connected world, will continue to have an impact on Christians. In its most positive sense, this globalization expresses the aspiration of human beings to become one family. However, globalization has further divided humanity

because in the present world order the forces of globalization work to the benefit of some and to the detriment of many.

84. In this context the ecumenical movement can be a seed of hope in a world that is divided economically, culturally, socially and politically. The joys and sorrows, hopes and despairs of all peoples are those of Christians as well. While respecting all human efforts to draw people together, the ecumenical movement can make its specific contribution to the unity of the human family by healing divisions among Christians. One response to globalization calls for the development of healthy mutual relationships between global and national social structures. A parallel ecumenical challenge is achieving common perspectives on the proper relationship between universal and local expressions of the church, and between unity and diversity. By showing that dialogue can resolve persistent differences, progress made on these ecclesiological questions can have a positive impact on persons responding to globalization.

85. Thus the continuing commitment to ecumenical dialogue not only fosters reconciliation among Christians, but is also a sign of humanity's deepest aspirations to become one family.

THE CONTINUING CHALLENGE OF CHRISTIAN RECONCILIATION

86. Some challenges relate specifically to the ecumenical movement itself.

87. While we rejoice in the achievements of the 20th century ecumenical movement we recognize that Christian reconciliation is far from complete. Ecumenical dialogue must continue in order to resolve serious divergences concerning the apostolic faith. These hinder the achievement of visible unity among Christians, the unity necessary for mission in a broken world.

88. Second, the ecumenical movement is important for Christians everywhere. Early in the ecumenical movement most participants came from Europe and North America, though the minority from other continents made an important impact in early ecumenical meetings, asserting that the disunity of the church was a sin and a scandal. As noted above many major divisions among Christians started in Europe, with European and American missionaries taking these to other continents in the course of their activities.

89. Today, however, dialogue participants come also from Africa, Asia, Latin America, Oceania and the Caribbean – and their contributions are significant. For many the ecumenical agenda is deemed to be less appropriate and urgent than their work for the provision of the basic needs of their communities. Yet many Christians realize that perpetuating divisions undermines the credibility of the one gospel, and that many of the issues that they face are indeed issues of unity and division. This gospel speaks to people in their different cultures and languages; and healing the wounds of division requires the efforts of Christians in every part of the world. The diversity among Christians around the world should receive much more attention in ecumenical dialogues in the 21st century.

90. Third, we have become aware of a changing Christian landscape. We acknowledge that some of the fastest-growing Christian communities are Evangelical and Pentecostal. Many if not most of these are not involved with the ecumenical movement and have neither contact with the WCC nor dialogue with the Roman Catholic Church. Indeed the very words "unity" and "ecumenical" are problematic for these communities.

Their major focus is on mission and they do not necessarily see this in the context of collaborating with other churches in a given region, even where these churches have been established for centuries. A challenge today is finding ways to make ecumenical dialogue more inclusive of these important Christian groups.

91. Fourth, bilateral dialogues have focused on matters needing resolution so that reconciliation between two Communions can be achieved. This must continue. But it may be helpful if some dialogues give more systematic attention to the Christian heritage shared by both East and West, as a frame of reference for all. Perhaps all dialogues, even as they address their own particular issues, could benefit by attending to this common Christian heritage.

THE CHALLENGE OF INTER-RELIGIOUS DIALOGUE

92. But although inter-religious dialogue cannot replace ecumenical dialogue, inter-religious dialogue is held among the world's religions. It seeks not to create one religion, but to enable collaboration among religions in fostering spiritual values to contribute to harmony in society, and to help to build world peace. Cooperation among Christians to promote inter-religious dialogue is necessary, even imperative, today. Recently religions have been abused in order to justify and even promote violence, or have been marginalized from efforts to build human community. Through ecumenical cooperation in inter-religious dialogue, Christians can support the world's religions in promoting harmony and peace.

93. Ecumenical dialogue and inter-religious dialogue must not be confused. While both are germane to the culture of dialogue, each has a specific aim and method. Ecumenical dialogue is held among Christians; it seeks visible Christian unity. It must continue because discord among Christians "openly contradicts the will of Christ" (*Unitatis Redintegratio*, 1) and must be overcome.

Conclusion

94. Since the 1967 JWG statement on dialogue, churches have participated in dialogue especially over the last decades of the 20th century. Ecumenical dialogue has opened new vistas, showing that despite long centuries of separation, divided Christians share much in common. Dialogue has contributed to reconciliation. The reception of dialogue results has been instrumental in bringing Christians together in various ways.

95. Now in the 21st century ecumenical dialogue continues with the same goals, but in a new context. Dialogue is still an instrument which Christians must use in their search for visible unity, a goal which still remains to be fulfilled. Dialogue continues to be an instrument to assist in reconciliation of divided Christians. In this time before us, the results of dialogue must be continually reviewed in the churches. Ecumenical dialogue has already helped to change relationships between churches. In the new context of a more globalized world, of a world of instant communication and abundant information, the church's task of proclaiming the word of God and salvation in Christ comes into unprecedented competition with proclamations of every sort of information aimed at capturing the human heart. All the more urgent in this time of history is the common witness to the gospel by Christians who can put aside their divisions and take up

common witness to the Lord, who prayed for his disciples "... that they may all be one... so that the world may believe" (John 17:21).

A NOTE ON PROCESS

After papers on dialogue were presented by Bishop Walter Kasper and Dr Konrad Raiser, the first plenary developed a series of issues to be considered in a study document on dialogue. A small drafting group consisting of Eden Grace, Dr Susan Wood, Msgr Felix Machado, Msgr John Radano, and Rev. Dr Alan Falconer, met in Cartigny, Switzerland (February 2003), and produced an initial draft. After discussions in the plenary in Bari, the text was further developed through email correspondence and at a one-day drafting session in September 2003 (Falconer, Radano, Dr Thomas Best). After further discussion at the JWG executive meeting in November 2004, Bishop David Hamid was asked to review the text for editorial consistency. The study document was adopted by the JWG plenary at Chania, Crete, in May 2004.

"Inspired by the Same Vision":
Roman Catholic Participation in National and Regional Councils of Churches
A JWG Study

I. The purpose of this document [1]

"The member churches of the World Council of Churches and the Roman Catholic Church are *inspired by the same vision* of God's plan to unite all things in Christ" (Common Understanding and Vision 4.11). One means of moving towards this vision has been membership and participation in councils of churches. After more than forty years of experience, the Joint Working Group is asking some basic questions about Catholic involvement in national and regional councils of churches and other ecumenical instruments. What works well? What is not working well? Why?

Many councils of churches are struggling with a variety of issues that, in some cases, also are vexing their member churches, such as trying to clarify anew purpose and direction; seeking to capture the imagination of new generations, and finding the financial resources needed to meet the expectations of members and the demands of common ministry. These issues have been considered in other contexts, and some references are listed at the conclusion of this text.

Because specific questions about Roman Catholic participation are being raised in the conciliar context, this document will examine some systemic issues that councils of churches are facing. Some of these are inherent in the very nature of councils. Some are new problems in a world that has changed significantly since councils first were formed. This is the contemporary environment in which we are shining a lens on particular questions.

When the Roman Catholic Church is a member of a national council of churches (NCC) or regional ecumenical organization (REO), what were the circumstances that facilitated membership? If concerns have surfaced, what are they? How are they being addressed? If signs of growth have resulted, what are they? How have they been nurtured? How has Catholic membership affected relationships among all the member churches?

When the Roman Catholic Church is not a member of an NCC/REO, what are some of the reasons? If concerns are cited, what are they? Have other ways, short of membership, been used to encourage participation? How has Catholic ecclesiology affected issues of participation and membership in councils? Has the possibility of participation by the Roman Catholic Church discouraged involvement by another church, and if so, for what reasons?

This study addresses one aspect of a multi-faceted ecumenical scene, and it is part of a series of periodic reflections about the nature and purpose of councils of churches. It was prepared by the Joint Working Group, the post-Vatican II instrument created to enhance relationships between the Roman Catholic Church and the World Council of Churches, in consultation with the leaders of NCCs and REOs, who offered valuable suggestions. We pray that it will strengthen appreciation for, understanding of, and participation in councils of churches.

II. Councils of churches and regional ecumenical organizations

When churches come together to form a council of churches, they consider the *theological basis* that becomes their organizing principle. Some of these bases have been Trinitarian (e.g. all churches who subscribe to the baptismal formula of "Father, Son, and Holy Spirit") or Christological (e.g. all churches which claim "Jesus Christ as Lord and Saviour"). Either implicit or explicit in this basis is a definition of their *purpose* in coming together through the council, and of the marks of membership. These bases, which vary somewhat, become the framework in which churches choose to apply for membership.

The ultimate aim of churches in the ecumenical movement is full visible Christian unity. Councils of churches are a privileged instrument by which churches can move towards this goal as they witness to a real, though incomplete unity in their service of the mission of the church.

At the same time, this study needs a working definition for councils of churches. One such definition has been given by a document produced by the Massachusetts Council of Churches:

> A council of churches is an institutional expression of the ecumenical movement, in which representatives of separated and autonomous Christian churches within a given area covenant together to become an enduring fellowship for making visible and effective the unity and mission of the church (*Odyssey Towards Unity*, p.30).

Sometimes membership in a council or conference includes not only churches, but also other ecumenical organizations. In these cases, the ecumenical body may use another name, such as "Christian Council", but the precise nature of membership is not necessarily self-evident from the organizational title alone.

1. ROMAN CATHOLIC PARTICIPATION IN NCCS: THE CURRENT SCENE

The participation of the Roman Catholic Church in national councils of churches is a phenomenon that has grown consistently since the Second Vatican Council. At the time of the Council, the Roman Catholic Church did not take part in any national council of churches, but at the present time, of approximately 120 national councils of churches, the Roman Catholic Church is a full member in 70.

The continents and regions where the Roman Catholic Church has membership in an NCC reflect a broad geographical spectrum. Europe, Africa, Oceania and the Caribbean make up the bulk of the regions in which the Roman Catholic Church is fully represented in national councils of churches. Elsewhere, the Roman Catholic Church is a member in some countries of Asia, Latin America and North America.

In several countries, partial or restricted membership has been achieved. In some countries, such as Zimbabwe and the Slovak Republic, the Roman Catholic Church enjoys observer or consultant status in the NCC. Elsewhere, as in the USA and in many Asian countries, the Roman Catholic Church, although still lacking any structural connection with other Christian churches through councils, has ongoing working relationships between the Catholic episcopal conference and the national council of churches. In the United States, for example, the Office of Ecumenical and Inter-religious Affairs of the US Conference of Catholic Bishops is a member of the Faith and Order commission of the National Council of Churches of Christ in the USA. In Chile, Argentina and Ecuador, "ecumenical fraternities" exist among church leaders. While not councils of churches, these fraternities serve as instruments of community.

Moreover, in many countries where the Roman Catholic Church is not a member of the NCC, Catholic dioceses are represented in the local or statewide councils of churches. For example, in Caracas, Venezuela, there is a council of the historical churches of which the Roman Catholic Church is a member. A less formal ecumenical association of churches, with Roman Catholic participation, exists in Mexico City. In the USA, of 41 state councils of churches, Catholic dioceses are members in at least thirteen state councils and participate as observers (variously defined) in at least six others.

Membership in 70 national councils does not show the full extent of Catholic participation. In 12 countries of the Middle East where there are no NCCs, the Roman Catholic Church is a full and active member of the regional body, the Middle East Council of Churches. At the fifth plenary assembly of the MECC in 1990, seven distinct churches in communion with Rome joined the MECC, forming the Catholic family of churches, along with the Orthodox, Oriental Orthodox and Evangelical families.

2. Catholic Participation in REOs: the current scene

Of the seven REOs associated with the World Council of Churches, the Roman Catholic Church is a member of three: the Caribbean Conference of Churches (CCC), the Pacific Conference of Churches (PCC), and the Middle East Council of Churches (MECC). In 1973, after a process of consultation and prayer begun in 1969, the Caribbean Conference of Churches was formed, with the Roman Catholic Church as a founding member. This was the first instance after the Second Vatican Council where the Roman Catholic Church entered into the process of founding a new regional ecumenical organization. The Pacific Conference of Churches was formed in 1966 and the Roman Catholic Church became a full member in 1976.

Participation of the Roman Catholic Church in a regional conference does not imply that the Catholic Church in every nation of that region also is a member of its respective national council. For example, although the Roman Catholic Church in some dioceses is a member of the regional Caribbean Conference of Churches (CCC), the

Catholic Church in Haiti, Puerto Rico, Cuba and the Dominican Republic is neither a member of the CCC nor of its respective national council of churches.

In regions where the Roman Catholic Church is not a member of the regional ecumenical organization, a good working relationship often exists between the REO and the continental association of Catholic episcopal conferences. In Europe, for example, a year after the Council of Bishops' Conferences in Europe (CCEE) was founded in 1971, the Conference of European Churches (CEC) established, in cooperation with the CCEE, a joint committee to promote collaboration. The two European bodies, the CEC and CCEE, following the encounters at Basel 1989 and at Graz 1997, in April 2001 signed a *Charta Oecumenica*, "Guidelines for CEC/CCEE Cooperation", which continues to have positive ripple effects in countries throughout the region.

In Asia, the Federation of Asian Bishops Conferences (FABC) and the Christian Conference of Asia (CCA) have intensified efforts at greater coordination and cooperation on common projects. Most recently, the two associations have undertaken cooperative projects on ecumenical formation, peace studies and inter-religious dialogue. Despite Pope John Paul II's appeals that the Roman Catholic Church in Asian countries should consider joining, where pastorally feasible, in ecumenical association with other churches, the churches in Asia have been relatively slow in responding. Only in Australia and Taiwan is the Roman Catholic Church a full member of the national council of churches. In Malaysia, the Catholic Church is not a member of the NCC, but takes part in the more inclusive association of the Christian Federation of Malaysia. It is perhaps because of this reluctance that the pope specifically urged, in his post-synodal exhortation *Ecclesia in Asia* of December 1999, that "the national episcopal conferences in Asia invite other Christian churches to join in a process of prayer and consultation in order to explore the possibilities of new ecumenical structures and associations to promote Christian unity" (§30).

The Australian experience is worth noting here. The Australian Council of Churches, formed in 1946, had Protestant, Anglican and eventually Orthodox membership. The Roman Catholic Church was not a member, nor were several Protestant churches. In 1988, the ACC members extended an invitation to churches that were not part of the ACC to work together towards creating a new structure that might more effectively express ecumenical relationships and serve the ecumenical movement in Australia. A planning group tried out ideas on prospective member churches and finally proposed that the ACC make way for a National Council of Churches in Australia (NCCA) with a rewritten constitution, revamped programme emphases, new decision-making processes and a more inclusive self-understanding. In 1994, the new NCCA came into being with 14 member churches: Eastern and Oriental Orthodox, Catholic and Protestant. The process has served as a catalyst for all the member churches to renew and deepen their ecumenical commitment.

Early relations between the Latin American REO, Consejo Latinoamericano de Iglesias (CLAI, Latin American Council of Churches), and the Consejo Episcopal Latinoamericano (CELAM, Latin American Episcopal Conference) were limited and often strained. Since 1995, however, the two organizations have reinitiated relations and have undertaken meetings, mutual visits, and a common project on the study of Pentecostal Christianity. The two organizations now are considering a proposal to form a permanent joint working group. In some countries of the region, such as Costa Rica, the churches are engaged in discussions that, it is hoped, will lead to an inclusive ecumenical association.

There are no projects in common between the 150-member All Africa Conference of Churches (AACC) and the Symposium of Episcopal Conferences of Africa and Madagascar (SECAM). However, the two organizations regularly extend invitations to each other to attend their plenary assemblies as observers.

III. Evolving attitude of the Roman Catholic Church to membership in NCCs

The Roman Catholic Church came late to the ecumenical movement. This is partially due to an attitude that ecumenism would constitute a compromise with error, partly because Catholics in the early part of the 20th century were hoping that other churches would "return" to the "fullness" of Christian faith which was to be found in the Catholic tradition. The turning point came with the 1964 Second Vatican Council Decree on Ecumenism, often referred to by its Latin title *Unitatis Redintegratio* (UR). Although the Decree on Ecumenism did not refer explicitly to councils of churches, the document laid the theological foundations for Catholic participation in such councils by recognizing the ecclesial character of other churches, repeatedly referring to them as "churches and ecclesial communities". Moreover, the Decree on Ecumenism shifts the focus on Christian unity for Catholics from an ecumenism of a return to Rome as the centre of the church to one in which Christ is seen "as the source and centre of ecclesiastical communion" (UR 20).

At the time of the Second Vatican Council, the Roman Catholic Church was not a member of any national council of churches, and the document *Unitatis Redintegratio* included no explicit encouragement to seek membership in NCCs. However, in a dramatic development in 1971, only seven years after the Decree on Ecumenism was promulgated, the Roman Catholic Church had joined the national council of churches in 11 countries. The number increased to 19 by 1975, to 33 by 1986, to 41 by 1993, to 70 in 2003 (or 82, if one includes the nations of the Middle East Council of Churches).

1. THE 1975 DOCUMENT, ECUMENICAL COLLABORATION

Before 1975, Catholic participation in NCCs was approved by the Holy See on a case-by-case basis, but no overall guidelines for participation had been published. The first explicit treatment came in 1975 in a document issued by the Pontifical Council for Promoting Christian Unity entitled *Ecumenical Collaboration at the Regional, National, and Local Levels* (EC). By then, the Roman Catholic Church was a member of the NCC in 19 countries.

This document is important for two reasons: (1) it elaborated the principles on which Catholic participation in councils of churches is based, and (2) it formed the basis of the position taken in the official 1993 *Guidelines*, which often simply restates the 1975 document. At the same time, the 1975 document must be understood in the context of an evolving attitude towards councils. Some elements regarding the nature and scope of ecumenical organizations as understood in *Ecumenical Collaboration* were subsequently modified in later documents.

Chapter 5 of the document, entitled "Considerations Concerning Council Membership", takes up the theological motivations for joining in ecumenical association with other Christian churches, as well as the practical difficulties to be kept in mind. The document holds that "since the Second Vatican Council's recognition of the ecclesial character of other Christian communities, the church has frequently called upon Catholics to cooperate not only with other Christians as individuals, but also with other churches and ecclesial communities as such" (5a). This association with other churches as churches, states the document, should not be seen as a purely pragmatic cooperation on matters of social and human concern, but should go beyond that to the more essential form of cooperation in the area of a common Christian witness of faith.

Membership in a council of churches implies "recognition of the council of churches as an instrument, among others, both for expressing the unity already existing among the churches and also of advancing towards a greater unity and a more effective Christian witness" (5b). Catholics and other Christians must not see their participation in councils of churches as the final goal of ecumenical activity, as though full Christian unity were to be achieved simply by joining a council of churches. Prayer and worship in common, cooperation in biblical translation and coordination of liturgical texts, joint statements on moral questions, and common responses to social issues of justice and peace are also steps towards unity and can be undertaken also in those regions where the Roman Catholic Church does not belong to a national or regional council, but such paths to unity can be facilitated and encouraged by Catholic participation in the council of churches.

This does not diminish the value of councils of churches, but rather underlines their importance in helping the churches to seek the fullness of unity that Christ desired among his disciples. As the document later concludes: "Among the many forms of ecumenical cooperation, councils of churches and Christian councils are not the only form, but they are certainly one of the more important" (6g). They play "an important role in ecumenical relations" and hence are to be taken seriously by all the churches.

The document seeks to relieve some of the theological disquiet that some Catholics might feel about joining a council of churches. Joining a council in which the Roman Catholic Church would find itself on equal footing with other bodies does "not diminish its faith about its uniqueness" (5b). The document cites the well-known statement of Vatican II that the unique church of Christ subsists in the Catholic Church (*Lumen Gentium* 8), and this uniqueness is not compromised by the church taking part, on equal footing with other churches, in a council at the national or regional level. Similar questions about the implications of membership in councils have been raised by other churches. These questions were addressed by the central committee of the World Council of Churches in Toronto in 1950, which stated that membership in a council of churches does not necessarily imply "that each church must regard the other member churches as churches in the true and full sense".

The document underlines that councils of churches are not churches; nor do they have the responsibility of churches to engage in conversations leading to full unity. As the document saw it in 1975, the scope of councils of churches is mainly in the practical realm, rather than in the dogmatic, a perspective that has since continued to evolve. In saying this, the Holy See does not forbid councils of churches to study together questions of "faith and order", and the document later notes that "it is normal that councils should want to discuss and reflect upon the doctrinal bases of the practical projects they undertake" (6h). Such discussions, it states, have "a deep importance in stimulating member churches to a deeper understanding of the demands of unity willed by Christ and to facing deadlocks in a new way" (5c). Nevertheless, it "is not the task of a council to take the initiative in promoting formal doctrinal conversations between churches. These belong to the immediate and bilateral contacts between the churches." Thus, in joining a council of churches, Catholics need not fear that they will be drawn into technical dogmatic discussions that they may not consider appropriate in this context.

The document regards the proper domain of councils of churches as principally that of practical collaboration, giving particular attention to social problems such as housing, health, relief, etc. (5e, ii). At times, the councils will feel called to make public statements on matters of common concern in areas of peace, social justice, human development, public welfare, and personal morality or social ethics. These may vary from broad statements of position to specific stands on concrete questions. They might examine a subject and point out its social and ethical ramifications, and they often will identify various approaches to treat problems. Even though such statements reflect the theological positions of the churches, they are not to be "considered as official utterances" (5d, i) made in the name of the churches.

In fact, as the document notes, the problematic nature of issuing joint statements is one that the member churches of a council must constantly keep in mind. It has given rise to much debate, tension and hard feelings in a number of councils and on rare occasions has led one or another member church to withdraw from a council. This does not mean that in councils, churches never should make public statements. They should realize, however, that full consensus is very difficult to achieve and that sincere respect must be granted to minority views (5d, iii). All this is to say that in a council of churches the integrity of each member church constantly must be considered, its individual positions honoured, and polarization avoided.

The document notes that when bishops conferences decide to join an NCC, they should not settle for superficial participation but should fully involve their local church. It is not enough simply to send delegates, but participation in a council should be integrated into the pastoral life and planning of Catholic dioceses. When the Roman Catholic Church joins a council, this must be accompanied by "constant ecumenical education of Catholics concerning the implications of such participation" (51).

In its "Pastoral and Practical Reflections for Local Ecumenical Action" in chapter 6 of EC, the Pontifical Council makes two further important points. First, each council of churches is unique and must be designed according to the needs in each nation. Churches should not simply adopt models that were found to be successful elsewhere (6a). Instead, after reflecting together on the needs and challenges of the churches in their region, they should create their own specific ecumenical relationship. The Holy See thus envisions a great deal of freedom for the churches in each region to form a council which accurately reflects the actual ecumenical relationships "on the ground" and enables the churches to express their unity in realistic service to society.

Second, as valuable as councils of churches are as instruments to express the unity which exists among Christians and to work towards fuller and deeper unity, the creation of new structures never can replace "the collaboration of Christians in prayer, reflection and action, based on common baptism and on a faith which on many essential points is also common" (6c). In other words, if the search for Christian unity is solely focused on structures, procedures and bureaucracy, the unity which councils seek to achieve will be minimal and the renewal which councils of churches can help their member churches bring to the whole Christian community will not be very profound. The deeper communion that should characterize Christian unity can only come from Christians' praying together, reflecting on the word of God in scripture together, thinking through social problems together, and actually working together in various aspects of the churches' life.

The aforementioned 1975 document on *Ecumenical Collaboration* was the first official instruction given by the Holy See on the question of Catholic membership in national and regional councils of churches. It noted with satisfaction that the Roman Catholic Church in many countries had decided to join NCCs or to create new ecumenical associations in which the Roman Catholic Church would take part. It pointed out possible problems that could arise and how many of the divisive issues could be foreseen and crises avoided. The document reassured Catholics throughout the world that joining a council of churches can be an important step towards working for Christian unity, expressing the unity which already exists due to our common baptism, and renewing the churches in their commitment to serve God in Christ and, in doing so, to be of service to a world reconciled to God.

Because of the increasing number of countries and regions where the Roman Catholic Church was participating in councils of churches, the Pontifical Council for Promoting Christian Unity and the World Council of Churches, within the framework of the Joint Working Group, convened three consultations (1971, 1986, 1993) to reflect on issues connected with national councils of churches.

In a message to the 1993 consultation, held in Hong Kong, Cardinal Edward Cassidy, then president of the Pontifical Council for Promoting Christian Unity, stressed a key aspect of the function of NCCs in the ecumenical search for unity. "National councils of churches", he stated, "as servants of unity play an important role in providing opportunities for strengthening the spirit of mutual understanding among member churches." The cardinal emphasized the human dimension, the value of councils to foster personal growth in commitment to Christian unity. He affirmed that in the NCCs, Christians of various churches come to know one another personally, discover a shared Christian commitment through common action, enrich one another by the distinctive elements of Christian life which their particular traditions have preserved and emphasized, and rediscover concretely their common faith in God by praying together in the name of Our Lord Jesus Christ.

2. THE 1993 "ECUMENICAL DIRECTORY"

In the same year as the Hong Kong consultation, the Pontifical Council for Promoting Christian Unity issued its revised guidelines for Christian ecumenism, entitled the *Directory for the Application of Principles and Norms on Ecumenism*. The 1993 Guidelines, as the document is popularly known, replaced the temporary *Ecumenical Directory* that had been called for by the Second Vatican Council and subsequently published in 1967 and 1970. The 1993 *Directory* treats questions of Catholic participation in councils of churches in paragraphs 166-71.

Many of the instructions contained in the 1993 *Directory* repeat those already given in the 1975 document on *Ecumenical Collaboration*, but on some key points, the *Directory* goes farther than the earlier document. This is particularly the case in welcoming, for the first time, Catholic participation in councils. The EC document treated the phenomenon of Catholic churches joining NCCs and REOs as a de facto reality in the ecumenical movement, calling councils an "important instrument" in the search for Christian unity. The *Directory* goes beyond this to welcome positively this phenomenon in church life as something to be desired (167).

The *Directory* distinguishes (166) between a "council of churches, composed of churches and responsible to the member churches", and a "Christian council", composed of churches as well as other Christian groups and organizations, such as Bible societies or YMCAs. This distinction reflects a tendency in some regions to form more inclusive Christian councils whose members not only would be churches but also other forms of Christian association. This development recognizes that in the effort to build Christian unity, other Christian groups and organizations often play a leading role.

The *Directory* does not recommend one form of association over the other, but leaves that decision to the authorities of local churches. These authorities, states the *Directory*, "will generally be the synod of Eastern Catholic churches or the episcopal conference (except where there is only one diocese in a nation)" (168). In preparing to make this decision, the Eastern synods or episcopal conferences "should be in touch with the Pontifical Council for Promoting Christian Unity". The *Directory's* careful phraseology underlines that the authority for joining councils rests with the local bishops through their synod or episcopal conference while, as in all matters affecting the universal church, the local churches should always communicate and consult with the Pontifical Council. What is involved is not a matter of "asking permission from Rome" but of acting in communion with the worldwide Roman Catholic Church.

The *Directory* notes various considerations that must accompany the decision to take part in a council of churches or Christian council. Local and national socio-political realities must be considered. Participation in the life of the council must not blur Catholic self-understanding as to its uniqueness and specific identity (169). In other words, there must be doctrinal clarity, especially in the area of ecclesiology, and ecumenical education should be provided for church members. In ecumenical dialogue, the Roman Catholic Church can propose its ecclesiology to other member churches, but should respect their proper ecclesiological self-understanding. At the same time, the Roman Catholic Church expects that its own theology of the nature of the church will be understood and respected by its partners.

The *Directory* repeats the view of the 1975 document that councils of churches and Christian councils do not contain within or among themselves the beginning of a new church that could replace the communion that now exists in the Roman Catholic Church. They must not proclaim themselves churches "nor claim an authority which would permit them to confer a ministry of word or sacrament". In fact, the concern that councils of churches not be regarded as a new "super-church" had already been a constant preoccupation of member churches since the first councils of churches appeared a century ago. The formation of councils among churches still divided from one another is but one instrument aimed at Christian unity, and it must be clearly distinguished from the effort to achieve structural and sacramental unity in the creation of united churches.

The *Directory* notes matters to be considered before the Roman Catholic Church either decides to join an existing NCC or to take part in the creation of a new association. Such considerations include the system of representation, voting rights, decision-making processes, manner of making public statements, and the degree of authority attributed to common statements (169.) Finally, the *Directory* repeats the counsel given in the 1975 document. Joining a council is a serious responsibility that should not be taken lightly. Membership implies responsibilities that are not fulfilled simply by becoming a member only in name. "The Catholic Church should be represented by well-qualified and committed persons" who are sincerely convinced of the importance of actively pursuing Christian unity and who are clearly aware of the limits to which they can commit the church without referring to the authorities who appointed them.

The increased acceptance and encouragement for Catholic participation in councils of churches by the Holy See since the time of the Second Vatican Council is evidence of a positive experience in observing the fruits of such ecumenical involvement. Most recently, in the 1995 document on ecumenical formation of Christians entitled *The Ecumenical Dimension in the Formation of Those Engaged in Pastoral Work*, the Pontifical Council for Promoting Christian Unity lists information about councils of churches as one of the "important pastoral and practical matters which should not be omitted from ecumenical formation, especially that of seminarians".

The emerging participation of the Roman Catholic Church in national and regional ecumenical organizations would not be complete without reference to the 1995 encyclical *Ut Unum Sint* ("That They May All Be One"), which strongly reaffirmed the commitment of the Roman Catholic Church to work actively for Christian unity. Although the encyclical did not refer explicitly to NCCs and REOs, the pope affirmed that "the relationships which the members of the Catholic Church have established with other Christians since the Council have enabled us to discover what God is bringing about in the members of other churches and ecclesial communities. This direct contact, at a variety of levels, with pastors and with the members of these communities has made us aware of the witness which other Christians bear to God and to Christ. A vast new field has thus opened up for the whole ecumenical experience, which at the same time is the great challenge of our time" (*UUS* 48.)

3. CONCLUDING COMMENTS ABOUT THE HISTORICAL SURVEY

Tracing the historical background of Catholic participation in national and regional councils of churches shows a progressive awareness in the Roman Catholic Church, beginning at the time of the Second Vatican Council, of the value of taking part in such associations. The Roman Catholic Church has come to see participation in NCCs and REOs as an important step in pursuing the Spirit-driven goal of Christian unity. Councils of churches are not the goal in the ecumenical search for the full unity, but they are an effective tool for following the Spirit's guidance towards full unity. The late Canadian theologian and ecumenist, Fr Jean-Marie Tillard, OP, sums up this grace-filled instrumentality of councils of churches as follows:

A council of churches makes a "loving dialogue" possible. By breaking the isolation and bringing about knowledge of each other, ecumenical encounter slowly erodes distrust, prejudices and traditional hatreds. While each church begins by hoping to impose its own views and confessional ambitions on the others, we find that among the members something gradually comes into being which triumphs over the interests and claims of each group. In learning to love one another, in the knowledge that diversities exist and in respect for them, we gradually learn the unity that God wants.

IV. Value and benefits of membership

1. WHAT CAN FACILITATE PARTICIPATION AND MEMBERSHIP

When a church joins a council, it brings along not only its rich heritage, but some painful memories as well. The original fear, apprehension or suspicion does not automatically disappear. A relatively long integration process may be needed to purify memories and develop trust, enabling the new member church to perceive itself and to be perceived by others as belonging comfortably to the council.

The process of integration is facilitated by instilling a feeling of *respect* for the integrity of the new member church. The church needs to feel confident that membership in the council, while causing it to change, will not force unsolicited alterations in its identity. This sense of reassurance is liable to generate deeper commitment to the common agenda of the members of the council and to encourage greater openness and participation on the part of the new member church. Such a feeling of security will allow the richness of yet another tradition to be shared. Both deep theological reflection and a clear understanding of ecumenical spirituality are vital factors in the process of journeying towards the visible unity of the church.

The success of this process also is fostered by the ability of the council members to *listen*. It hinges on their openness, their readiness to accept and value differences, their ability to be truly inclusive. Such an attitude is bound to lead to greater sharing in the decision-making process, always taking into consideration minority views. When making decisions, no matter how insignificant they may appear, it is always preferable to aim at consensus rather than to risk alienating member churches who may have different perspectives.

The way the council is formed and the manner in which churches are represented can make a difference in how member churches perceive their role in the decision-making mechanism. For example, if the member churches are represented according to their numerical importance some may feel that their vote will not make a difference. As a result they may feel alienated from the decision-making process. Such feelings are bound to influence negatively their sense of belonging to the council.

If the representation is made, however, according to other criteria, such as the "families of churches", where each family is equally represented, independently of numbers of faithful, no member church will feel at a disadvantage when it comes to influencing decisions. Moreover, the family model may enable the member churches within a family to grow into closer relationships and cooperation with each other. In addition, this model may facilitate the entrance of a church as part of a family when it would be uncomfortable in joining a council that did not have a family structure.

When a new member feels accepted, integrated, valued and represented in the decision-making process, a deeper feeling of belonging can grow. Each member feels more ready to participate in common projects both at the level of leadership and at the grassroots, where the rapprochement remains the ultimate objective of the ecumenical journey.

Becoming part of a council of churches may enhance a church's renewal, rescue it from isolation, strengthen its awareness of the common calling, increase the effectiveness of its service, and encourage ecumenical initiatives by its people locally.

Flexibility in council structures facilitates participation and membership. For example, each member should feel free to engage in bilateral dialogue outside the structure of the council, while remaining part of it.

The factors named above are practical. They point to aspects of healthy dialogue – a subject that is being explored by a separate study on dialogue conducted by the Joint Working Group. More important, however, are the spiritual and theological motivations of member churches. By joining an ecumenical association, each member demonstrates a willingness to allow the Spirit to witness to the existing unity of the church and an intention to cooperate to further its visible unity.

2. WHAT CAN HELP MEMBER CHURCHES LIVE OUT STATED AIMS

Like any institution, councils of churches derive their strength partly from the quality of the people involved. The contribution of each member church depends a great deal on the capacity of its representatives – on their ecumenical formation and commitment. The ecumenical movement is a journey of the whole community and not of an elite that represents it.

Official representatives to councils should be in close contact with the leaders and people of the churches they represent. Unless the heads of churches are informed about the process and encourage it, their participation could cause internal divisions and discourage communication with the people in the pews.

When people join together through any association it makes a significant difference to the general atmosphere if people get along well and enjoy working together – hence, the importance of the development of a spirit of fellowship. An attitude of trust and readiness for true dialogue are vital starting points for the realization of the stated objectives of the council. Unless members trust each other they cannot easily be committed to the same aims, especially when the commitment involves deep theological convictions. And unless the aims are based on such acknowledged theological convictions, the partners in a council will not be able to get far in the realization of their goals in their ecumenical journey.

Thus, members should have a common mission in their journey towards unity. Ecumenical progress is thwarted by those who have hidden agendas, seek personal benefits, or entertain human ambitions. Such an approach goes counter to common witness.

In conclusion, participants in ecumenical work cannot make progress unless the persons involved succeed in creating healthy human relationships among themselves and a deep relationship with God. Differences should not be hidden. Ecumenical progress cannot be promoted by avoiding real issues or seeking easy solutions to vexing problems. The ecumenical journey is always a journey of mending relationships, of healing the wounds of division and reconciling memories in order to seek together unity in Jesus Christ through the enlightenment of the Holy Spirit.

Witnessing to the visible unity of the church starts with prayerful journeying together towards an encounter with God, towards a deeper transformation in order to manifest God's presence in the world through the church. In praying together, Christians encounter the Triune God who brings about the gradual transformation of the community into a true family of Christ's disciples. This process is enhanced through a deep encounter among the various members of the council in which they discover each other's wealth of tradition and special spiritual experience. Listening to the Spirit speaking to the churches helps dissipate prejudice – at times, even hatred. It produces greater trust and leads to growth. This is perhaps the most eloquent witness of a Council to the visible unity of the church.

3. WHAT SHOULD BE CELEBRATED

Ecumenical awakening is one of the most important developments in the history of the church during the 19th and the 20th centuries. Some Christians began to be aware of the value of cooperation among the churches. Protestants were the first to take steps towards creating ecumenical organizations intended to overcome divisions among Christians. In 1910, the international missionary conference at Edinburgh marked the beginning of the modern ecumenical movement, and from this the churches together continued to cooperate in mission through the International Missionary Council to bring churches together to explore divisive theological issues through Faith and Order; and to engage in reflection and action on political, social and economic matters through Life and Work. In 1920 the Ecumenical Patriarchate issued an encyclical entitled "Unto the Churches of Christ Everywhere", inviting Christians to create a fellowship of churches. In the same year the bishops of the Anglican Communion issued an "Appeal to All Christian People" to manifest unity by "gathering into fellowship all who profess and call themselves Christians, within whose visible unity all the treasures of faith and order, bequeathed as a heritage by the past to the present, shall be possessed in common, and made serviceable to the whole body of Christ". The rapid development of ecumenical associations, notably the creation of the World Council of Churches in 1948, underlines the importance the churches have ascribed to working for the full visible unity of the church. In 1900 there were no national councils of churches, but by the year 2000 the number had grown to 103.

Since the Second Vatican Council the Roman Catholic Church has joined a large number of ecumenical associations. This rapprochement, along with the engagement in bilateral dialogue with a wide range of churches and ecclesial communions in both East and West, has led to the signing of Christological agreements with some of the Oriental churches. Dialogue with the Lutherans recently produced significant progress shown in the Joint Declaration on the Doctrine of Justification. The efforts of the Anglican-Roman Catholic Commission (ARCIC) have led to the publication of the "Gift of Authority". Although not a joint declaration, this document offers valuable insights for the future directions of the ecumenical movement.

With councils of churches as their principal instruments, the churches are building relationships with each other through which they are:

– growing in mutual respect, understanding and trust;

– dissipating many prejudices through learning to pray in each other's words, singing each other's songs, reading scripture through each other's eyes;

– offering service in Christ's name to those who are in need, locally and far away;

– giving common witness to the gospel and working together for human dignity;

– listening to and learning through each other's insights into matters of faith and life over which they have been divided;

– holding Christ's people together, even when the world's pressures would tear them apart (*CUV*, 3.9).

Relationship building affects all those involved. One church encountering another may find that it wants to reflect afresh on its own identity, its own thinking, its own Christian commitment to unity. Ecumenical ties bring many benefits, some quite unexpected.

V. Some issues and concerns

1. WHAT'S IN A NAME?

Names can matter. A name says something about how the churches perceive their life together. When a Catholic bishops conference joins a national council of churches, a name change may dramatize that the churches are making a fresh beginning together. The new name may symbolize new intentions and new reality – an awareness that the culture of the council will be transformed as new churches live into new relationships through the council. Thus, names are important, but context, history and vision will determine the choice in a given place.

Most call themselves *councils* of churches. Some call themselves *conferences* of churches. Others have adopted names like *churches together* or *Christian fellowships*. In fact, the vast majority of national ecumenical bodies with Catholic membership use the phrase "council of churches" in their name. The phrase "Christian council" sometimes, though not always, indicates that other ecumenical organizations (e.g., Bible societies, Church Women United, YMCA and YWCA) also may be members.

The Roman Catholic Church's relationship to national and regional councils of churches may take one of several forms: full membership, observer status, ongoing collaboration, occasional cooperation. Although some concerns are felt more acutely when Roman Catholic Churches are involved, other churches and ecclesial communities may experience, to varying degrees, the same problems. Councils within a country (state, province, city) may have similar experiences. Thus, awareness of and attention to these concerns may enable greater and better participation in a council, not only by the Roman Catholic Church but also by the other churches.

2. ISSUES OF AUTHORITY

In national settings, the Conference of Catholic Bishops has the authority to make the decision about joining a national council of churches. In a diocesan setting, the bishop makes the decision. The attitude towards councils of churches taken by an individual bishop or bishops conference can either encourage or inhibit participation in a council and the movement towards membership. Just as in any church, a few ecumenically committed bishops can stimulate action by the whole bishops conference. Furthermore, positive ecumenical experiences in the diocesan context may predispose bishops to consider membership in a national council. In Australia, for example, Catholic membership in some state councils of churches preceded consideration of participation by the Australian Catholic Bishops Conference. Membership in the National Council of Churches in Australia in turn stimulated other Catholic bishops to lead their dioceses into state councils of churches. The positive process was circular and expansive.

Once a Catholic Conference becomes a member of a council of churches, entering fully into the life of the ecumenical body, the relationships cannot be reversed lightly, without serious provocation. On rare occasions, such situations do arise. In 1998, the Catholic Bishops Conference in New Zealand withdrew from membership in the Conference of Churches in Aotearoa-New Zealand (CCANZ) after it became apparent that the method of representation did not afford the bishops the degree of necessary comfort with policies and practices of the new structure. The new body had set out to be a different type of council, seeing itself as a forum for various kinds of interest groups and causes as well as for the member churches who were financing it. From the outset some predicted that there would be difficulties for Catholic members. The Lutheran church in New Zealand experienced similar problems and withdrew from membership in the Conference in 1994.

Since the withdrawal of the Lutheran and Roman Catholic churches, religious leaders (especially Anglican, Presbyterian and Catholic) have made considerable effort to develop greater trust and to seek ways of working together even if their experience in CCANZ was not satisfactory. The Anglican and Roman Catholic bishops have met regularly for over a decade. They have expressed the sadness felt by many about CCANZ. Recently, CCANZ decided to conclude its organization, primarily because the remaining number of member churches is so small. At the same time, the possibility of a new body is being explored. This would give Catholics, Lutherans and Baptists (who had not joined CCANZ) a way back into a new ecumenical entity. As of this writing, plans for a new, inclusive council are scheduled to be unveiled by September 2004, when CCANZ will meet for its final annual forum.

This leads to the examination of another aspect of authority when churches are members of a council of churches. Who actually can speak for the churches at the ecumenical table? With what weight? The variations in ecclesiological self-understanding among churches sometimes are baffling to members, since all churches may be puzzled by polities and structures of authority that differ from their own. In the Catholic context the bishops need to trust that the concerns and policies of their church are reflected by the Catholic representatives, respected by other member churches and by the professional staff of a council of churches. In fact, this is true for leaders of other churches, as well.

Concerns have emerged about who, when, and on what basis the churches may speak together through a national council of churches. Members of the World Council of Churches faced these concerns early on and, in the 1950 Toronto statement clarified the limits of Council authority. Fr Yves Congar and other Catholic theologians were consulted prior to the drafting of the Toronto text.

To the degree that councils of churches and their professional leaders have honoured the policies articulated in Toronto, they have quelled fears that a council could become a "super-church", acting apart from or above its members. The WCC constitution addresses issues of authority as follows:

> The World Council shall offer counsel and provide opportunity for united action in matters of common interest.

> It may take action on behalf of constituent churches only in such matters as one or more of them may commit to it and only on behalf of such churches.

The World Council shall not legislate for the churches nor act for them in any manner except as indicated above or as may hereafter be specified by the constituent churches.

Recognizing the complexities involved in issues of authority does not necessarily solve problems, but an awareness of the dynamics may help. In the final analysis, many issues of authority depend on styles of leadership and modes of working together. When the style is relational, even when hard issues surface where tensions are high, people can rely on the human connections they have developed to consult together to seek the will of Christ.

3. PROPER PREPARATION FOR MEMBERSHIP

Experience has shown that by paying careful attention at the outset to issues of representation and decision-making processes, councils can minimize the problems in these areas that could arise later on. Serious preparation for membership in a council is an important factor leading to the successful functioning of all councils, both those with and without Catholic membership. For example, both the Canadian and Brazilian Catholic conferences of bishops were engaged for over a dozen years before they became full members of their national councils.

The Canadian Catholic Conference of Bishops joined an already established council, the Canadian Council of Churches, as full members in 1997 after a lengthy process that began in the 1970s when the two organizations worked together on social justice issues. In 1984, the Catholic Church applied for associate membership. The Conference of Bishops became an associate in 1986 with the intention of becoming a full member in 1997. The differences between the two types of membership were technical, i.e., not holding the office of president or general secretary, and not voting on constitutional issues.

The Canadian Catholic Conference of Bishops and the Canadian Council of Churches saw full membership as a concrete expression of greater commitment to the ecumenical movement. The inclusion of the Roman Catholic Church also brought an increased French dimension into what had been a largely English-speaking council. Before becoming full members, the Canadian Catholic Conference made a serious review of the constitution and by-laws of the council. The council resolved the concern about the organization being perceived as a "super-church" by frequently expressing itself as a forum "in which churches meet as churches to decide together on common agenda". Particular attention was given to making public statements and to identifying the authority those public statements would have.

The Brazilian council of churches began to take shape in the enthusiastic atmosphere following the Second Vatican Council when Catholics joined with other Christian leaders to form a council. The leaders met in Rio de Janeiro and in other major cities. These ecumenical efforts throughout the country resulted in the formation of the Brazilian National Council of Churches in 1982. The membership includes the Lutheran Evangelical, Episcopal, Methodist, United Presbyterian, Syrian Orthodox, Catholic and Christian Reformed churches.

4. FORMS OF REPRESENTATION, MODELS OF MEMBERSHIP

In countries where Roman Catholics form the majority of Christians, one of the arguments often given to explain the lack of Catholic membership in councils is that, by becoming "one church among others", the Roman Catholic Church would be conceding identity and leadership to a group of small churches. On the other hand, numerically small churches in such nations and regions also may be hesitant to welcome membership of the Roman Catholic Church, which they feel would dominate the council by its very size and social presence.

Such apprehensions could explain, for example, the absence of Catholic membership in church councils in much of Latin America and areas of Mediterranean Europe where Roman Catholics are predominant. Another factor affecting membership is that historically some councils of churches in predominantly Catholic contexts were established by minority churches precisely in order to help and support each other. In such situations, the prospects for Catholic membership may be difficult to accept for both the majority and minority churches.

Another model has been adopted by churches in Great Britain and Ireland – the churches together model. It is based on the model of "consensus". No action is taken unless and until there is agreement. The churches no longer delegate tasks to outside bodies, but each church takes responsibility in conjunction with other churches. This model very often includes as a full member the Roman Catholic Church (e.g. CTBI, ACTS, CTE in the United Kingdom). Often, in this model, there is a dual pattern of meetings of church leaders and a wider assembly of church representatives to pursue the agenda, and to provide an opportunity for mutual accountability.

Although these are real concerns, some councils, including those in regions with Catholic majorities such as Austria, Madagascar and Hungary, have found creative solutions which permit the various member churches to feel adequately represented. Several models of representation have been tried, and no single model can be said to be superior to others. It cannot be presumed that a solution that has worked well in one council can for that reason be applied successfully elsewhere. In whatever form of representation is devised, the main consideration always must be to ensure that all member churches are satisfied that their voices will be heard and that their views can find a proper forum, and that no church feels that its concerns will be ignored or over-ridden by the others.

Concerns of representation are not limited to Catholic participation. It is a perennial challenge for all church councils to find a structure that both adequately reflects ecumenical relationships and provides an arena for free discussion and interaction. In virtually every nation and region, the complexion of membership varies greatly. A church that represents the vast majority of Christians in that region can be uneasy if it feels that small churches will have the ability to push through legislation and projects on a "one church, one vote" basis. Conversely, small churches often will not feel comfortable in a structure that permits one or two large churches to dominate the council and force their will on other members.

On these bases, various councils have sought to devise systems of representation according to their particular needs and relationships. For example, the Uruguay Council of Christian Churches, with eight member churches (Anglican, Armenian, Catholic,

Evangelical, Lutheran, Methodist, Pentecostal and Salvation Army) has adopted a direct form of representation, with no adjustments made for church size.

By contrast, in the Canadian Council of Churches, representation of the 18 members reflects church size: three representatives from large churches, two from mid-sized, and one from small churches. Membership size of churches also determines Brazilian representation in that council's decision-making structures. The Brazilian council also rotates the presidency among leaders from different churches.

Representation based on "families of churches" rather than the size of church membership is used in other countries and regions with Catholic participation. The council of churches in France (CECEF), perhaps one of the few formed through the initiative of the Roman Catholic Church, has three co-presidents and three co-secretaries (one each from the Catholic episcopal conference, from the Protestant federation, from the assembly of Orthodox bishops). Its 16 member churches are composed of two Armenian Apostolic, five Catholic, three Orthodox, and five Protestant representatives, and an Anglican observer.

The Swedish Christian council, newly reconstituted in 1993, is based on four families, despite the fact that the Evangelical Lutheran Church of Sweden enrolls over 80 percent of the Christian population of the country. The families are the Lutheran, Orthodox, Catholic, and free-church families.

The family model also is followed by the Middle East Council of Churches, which is made up of four families: Catholic, Eastern Orthodox, Evangelical and Oriental Orthodox churches. In this context, the family model ensures that each of the major ecclesial traditions can feel that its position in the council will be taken seriously, that factors which make some churches historically and theologically "closer" to others will be recognized within the council structure, and that no single church or group of churches will be able to dominate leadership and decision-making processes.

The family model also has its drawbacks. Churches within a family may hold different positions on various issues. Concentrating on family relationships at the expense of building broader ecumenical relations can result in introversion and self-isolation. At times, the "family" can be an artificial construct, bringing together churches into families in which they are not comfortable. Moreover, some churches may not fit well into any given family, or there might be internal disagreement among church members about the family to which they belong. A church might see itself in one family, but not be regarded as such by others in that family. The family system on occasion even can result in a church being denied membership in the council. For example, one of the factors which has thus far prevented the Assyrian Church of the East from being accepted as a member of the Middle East Council of Churches is the lack of agreement over the family to which the church should belong.

Christian charity and the desire for fairness demand that all member churches be willing to give up some measure of autonomous decision-making and independent action for the sake of common voice and endeavour. Moreover, any form of representation only will work well when the churches have a measure of trust that other members are not seeking to manipulate council structures for their own purposes. It has been the experience of some councils that the prayerful deliberations that lead to determining the type of representation to be followed have been a valuable educational exercise and one that has occasioned greater fellowship and understanding.

5. DECISION-MAKING

Initially, most councils used the parliamentary, majority vote method for making decisions. More recently, many councils are employing methods that use discernment and consensus as being more compatible with the goal of promoting communion among their members. A common understanding of consensus is the achievement of a decision acceptable to all members. In some cases this agreement may be unanimous. More often, the consensus involves a decision that members can accept without objection. If councils cannot reach a consensus, other actions that may be taken are to record the various opinions, to postpone the decision or to refer the issue for study rather than for action. The understanding and practice of consensus must be agreed upon and accepted by all members. It is important, therefore, to have written protocols and to follow them.

Acceptance of consensus formation as the main pattern of decision-making does not imply that recourse must never be taken to parliamentary-style voting. Some issues (e.g., disbursement of funds, the appointment of officials) simply cannot be achieved by consensus.

Some councils are moving towards a more sophisticated understanding of consensus that might be expressed by the term "differentiated agreement". Derived from the experience of bilateral dialogues, differentiated agreement indicates a consensus on basic truths, although differences of language, theological elaboration and emphasis might remain. In a differentiated agreement, each church formulates the agreed-upon statement according to its own categories and understanding of its theological import.

A consensus style of decision-making often does not enable a council to make a prophetic statement in a timely manner. Some councils refer matters to individual member churches for separate actions. Other councils develop principles on particular issues on which the churches agree. Responses then can be made flowing from these principles. Potentially divisive and strongly prophetic positions only should arise from a profound spirit of prayer. A prayerful, discerning attitude and process may enable either a consensus to be reached or a respectful acceptance by the church that is unable to act on a particular issue.

6. PUBLIC STATEMENTS

Perhaps the factor that causes the greatest reluctance for churches that are considering membership in church councils concerns apprehension about public statements. Churches fear that their name will be used against their will to endorse causes with which their church is not in agreement or to protest issues on which they feel the churches should maintain a prudent silence. They may have heard of previous instances where churches were embarrassed by the actions of a majority of member churches, committees or general secretaries whose positions were announced publicly without prior consultation or full agreement of all member churches.

Differences in ecclesiology lie at the root of some difficulties in making public statements. Some churches at the local or national level may state their position on matters of importance without consulting other bodies. Catholic positions are to be in agreement with the magisterial teaching of the universal church and to reflect the position of their national bishops conferences. For the Orthodox, statements must be in accord with Orthodox theology.

In some cases, such as on questions of abortion or homosexuality, the problem is theological; some churches are concerned lest they appear to take positions contrary to the wider community's understanding of the Christian faith. In other cases, the churches may be concerned about the political implications of public positions, particularly in instances where government policy is criticized. In the case of many controversial issues, such as the death penalty, support or condemnation of war, or reproductive technology, opinion within the individual churches itself may be divided, with various interpretations of Christian teaching put forth by segments of the local community. A public statement on which many church members agree may be hotly contested by others.

There is no easy answer to the question of public statements, and disputes over the issue sometimes have led churches to withdraw from membership when no acceptable solution can be found. Most churches agree that there are times when the Christian conscience is united on an issue that, therefore, must be stated clearly in a public way. In fact sometimes a church's collective conscience will demand that it take a prophetic stance on controversial issues that run contrary to public opinion. Extensive ongoing consultation can minimize the possibility of conflict, dissension and hard feelings.

Councils must resist the culture of the instant statement, despite the pressures to the contrary. On the one hand, in today's fast-paced world, with instant modes of communication and a demanding news media, the insistence by member churches on full consultation and consensus may mean that the churches' voice on major ethical issues will be muted. On the other hand, members of councils have found that taking adequate time to deliberate may be frustrating, but it also can result in statements that are more clear and thoughtful. When there is open, continuous communication between council officials and the leaders of member churches, questions about which issues are likely to raise controversy or to be divisive become second nature to the conciliar staff.

Most councils issue statements only when they have achieved unanimity. If unanimous agreement is not possible, the statement may not be issued in the name of the council, because the council speaks not for itself but for every church that is a member. In such situations, it always must be clarified whether council officials speak as members of the council or as the official representatives or heads of their churches. Those who support the action may sign in the name of their church, while the minority may indicate their objections and their reasons for not signing the statement.

It also is important to honour a reluctance of members to make conflicts public unless external factors, such as media scrutiny, force the situation. Therefore, councils may need a common understanding of a procedure for relating to the media. For example, if one leader receives a call that could be contentious, prior agreement on the need for consultation before any public statements are made provides a level of trust and confidence among members.

7. FINANCES

Because councils of churches are their members, this fact should be reflected in a fair and equitable distribution of the costs entailed by membership. As churches, themselves, are challenged economically, these challenges are felt keenly in the budgets of councils of churches.

When councils of churches are especially dependent on outside funding, they find themselves being constrained by the expectations of funding agents who try to determine the programme of the council, regardless of the needs and perspectives of the member churches within a country.

When the Roman Catholic Church considers becoming a member of an NCC or REO, questions of and fears about cost inevitably arise (as they do for any potential member). When the Roman Catholic Church is predominant in size, members and budget, questions arise about how to work out an equitable resolution to financial responsibilities. The issue is not insurmountable, nor should it be used as a convenient excuse for avoiding the membership question, but it needs to be acknowledged forthrightly.

8. Ecumenical formation

Although much has been accomplished by the churches in describing "the nature of the unity we seek", not all share this vision to the same extent. Even in the midst of these ambiguities, however, all churches have a crying need to foster ecumenical formation among religious leaders, teachers, clergy and laity. Many are talking about the need for ecumenical formation. How to translate perceived need into effective action is a vexing challenge – one that councils of churches must face as they seek to juggle the sometimes conflicting demands of inclusivity, expertise and historical memory.

Attentiveness to ecumenical formation is especially important for those who are asked to serve as official representatives in ecumenical contexts such as councils of churches. The Holy See has urged that Catholic representatives have adequate ecumenical education and experience in order to express well the Catholic position, and to be aware of the history and methodology of the ecumenical movement.

All churches face the challenge of finding systemic ways to promote ecumenical formation for religious leaders, clergy, pastoral workers, and laity. The Pontifical Council for Promoting Christian Unity addressed this issue in its text, *The Ecumenical Dimension in the Formation of Those Engaged in Pastoral Work.* Seminary education is an obvious place to look for it. Ecumenical consortia of seminaries and theological faculties also could be the locus for ecumenical education.

A variety of institutes provide formation. Some of these include the Ecumenical Institute at Bossey (Switzerland), the Irish School of Ecumenics (Dublin), the Tantur Institute (Jerusalem), St Thomas University (Rome and Bari) and the Centro Pro Unione (Rome). Some councils of churches also have offered formal study. For example, the Christian Conference of Asia has offered courses of ecumenical formation for more than 25 years.

What has been lacking thus far, however, are adequate structures for monitoring and accountability of the ecumenical mandate *within* churches. Thus, we pose some questions:

- What processes are in place to encourage regular reporting back to the churches by their ecumenical official representatives?
- What mechanisms might be created to encourage the teaching of ecumenics by ecumenical teams? For example, when courses on the history, theory and practice of ecumenism are offered, are they planned, promoted, supported and taught in cooperation with ecumenical partners?
- When church leaders meet internally, do they make time to consider the ecumenical implications of their actions? Do they consider the significance of ecumenical texts for their churches?

- When churches reconsider previous positions in the process of theological development, do they make efforts to share the process and its outcome with other churches?
- In what ways can the churches better recognize, encourage and support those who have proposed fresh ecumenical initiatives?

9. ALTERNATIVES TO FULL PARTICIPATION

The ultimate aim of churches in the ecumenical movement is full, visible Christian unity. Councils of churches are a privileged instrument by which churches can move towards this goal. Thus all churches are encouraged to enter into prayerful reflection through which the Holy Spirit might lead them into membership in a council of churches as a step along the way towards full, visible unity.

For a variety of reasons, membership may not seem possible or advisable at a particular time in a given context. When this is the case, some alternatives may be considered. These include the following.

Ongoing structured cooperation: For example, the Christian Conference of Asia and the Federation of Asian Bishops Conferences have an agreed policy of reciprocal invitations to participate in each other's activities, have a joint ecumenical planning committee, and hold joint staff meetings that lead to the common planning and execution of projects. In the United States, the Ecumenical and Inter-religious Affairs Committee of the US Conference of Catholic Bishops is a member of the Faith and Order commission of the National Council of the Churches of Christ in the USA, although it is not a member of the NCCC. In Europe, the Conference of European Churches and the CCEE have been working together for a long time on a structured basis on various ecumenical projects, most recently in promoting the Charta Oecumenica.

Occasional cooperation on specific projects: An example might be taken from Sweden, where the Swedish Council of Churches worked together with the Roman Catholic Church in Sweden to prepare for the visit of the pope in 1989, at a time when the Catholic Church was still not a member. Inspired by the friendships formed and the cooperation achieved on that occasion, the Roman Catholic Church asked to be a founding member in the reorganized Swedish Christian Council.

Observer status: Some years ago, the CCEE nominated two permanent observers on the Conference of European Churches Commission on Churches in Dialogue. The Anglican church has observer status in the Council of Christian Churches in France, as does the Roman Catholic Church in the Zimbabwe Council of Churches.

Shared participation in ecumenical gatherings beyond one's own nation: At the second ecumenical European assembly in Graz, Austria, in 1997, some representatives of Orthodox, Greek Catholic and Protestant churches from Romania worked together ecumenically for the first time.

10. BILATERAL DIALOGUES AND RELATIONSHIPS

Some councils have experienced a lessening of physical presence and financial support from council members who give priority to bilateral dialogues, common agreements or mergers. All these relevant venues are means of promoting the one ecumenical movement and can best be viewed as complementary rather than competing.

The numerous Catholic international bilateral forums focus on specific doctrinal issues that continue to divide the churches. Some national bilateral dialogues have provided significant theological and biblical resources for these international dialogues. Also, bilateral dialogues have allowed Catholics to have formal conversations with evangelicals.

Some churches are moving towards fuller communion through specific bilateral or multilateral agreements. Also, some churches are developing closer relations with their worldwide community. Such movements necessarily involve the participating churches in intensive dialogue on a wide range of theological, ecclesial and other issues. When integrated into councils, these insights can be powerful means of deepening theological discussion and renewal to promote Christian unity. They also can provide opportunities for fresh opportunities and insights when viewed from the multilateral context that a council affords.

Since whatever occurs between two churches affects all churches in the ecumenical movement, churches engaged in bilateral dialogues should seek wherever possible to include observers from other churches in their dialogues. They also should encourage all participants to make detailed reports to the broader ecumenical community.

VI. Some questions to consider

Beyond issues explored elsewhere in this document, the possibility of the Roman Catholic Church becoming part of an existing ecumenical body confronts all concerned, the council's member churches no less than the prospective newcomer, with searching questions. For churches that are already members, the challenge is not only the organizational one of accommodating one more delegation around the ecumenical table, but also presents other questions:

• Are they willing to examine critically what previously may have been a Protestant conciliar culture, and to alter that culture when Catholics become members?
• Are they sufficiently aware of Catholic documents and teachings about ecumenism?
• Do they appreciate the variety of ecclesiological assumptions that will be around the expanding table and the ways these differences will impact their ecumenical deliberations?

Catholic bishops conferences, too, may find some assumptions challenged:

• Are their members sensitive to the significantly different history of ecumenism as it has been experienced by Orthodox churches and churches of the Reformation?
• Can they deal positively with a Protestant approach to ecumenism that sometimes may seem practically oriented, cooperatively driven and less interested in addressing doctrinal differences between the churches?

And for each church involved even more fundamental questions arise:

• Is its approach to the prospect of a more inclusive council driven by self-centred considerations, a "what's in it for us?" approach – or by the gospel imperative?
• Is the church prepared to be enriched by the gifts that each church brings to the ecumenical table?
• How can we, through our participation in the council of churches, further the mission of the church of Jesus Christ?

VII.   Concluding observations

At one level a council of churches is a structure, with all the accoutrements that go with structures – memberships, constitutions, decision-making procedures, policies, programmes, budgets and, probably, staff. Structure matters. As shown above, a well-functioning council of churches can do much to further the quest for Christian unity. Functioning badly, it may slow or even obstruct the quest.

But at a deeper, more important level, a council is a set of *relationships* between still-divided churches. Under God, they are the principal actors in the ecumenical movement. A council is not primarily an organization, or staff, or programmes. It is the *member churches*, in their shared commitment to God and to one another, attempting to respond together to the pressure of their common calling.

Such ties between churches find expression in many ways, not least in the relationships between the people who lead and represent them. Hence the emphasis in these pages is on the importance of fostering mutual understanding, respect, forbearance, trust. Hence the emphasis, too, is on making decisions in ways that will strengthen such relationships and foreshadow the reconciliation for which the churches yearn. Relationship-building, for any council of churches, always takes priority over the adoption of policies, the running of programmes, the administering of an institution. At least, it should. Ecumenical structures, like others, are tempted at times to a certain introversion. If finances are inadequate, for example, or policies are contentious, a focus on organizational problems is likely to distract attention from the very movement such structures were created to foster.

Likewise, even the best council loses something vital when a pioneering generation passes, to be succeeded by church leaders and representatives who inherit commitments over which others had to struggle. Like baptismal or marriage vows, the ecumenical promises churches make to each other, and to God, would benefit from continuous renewal in the Holy Spirit.

Increased Catholic participation in NCCs and REOs may provide a stimulus for just such renewed commitment by churches already involved in councils, no less than by those considering membership. It comes as a reminder, yet again, that the gospel of reconciliation requires a visibly reconciled faith community, so that the churches dare not rest content with the status quo. Above all, it comes as a sign of hope, a reminder that God in Christ and the Holy Spirit has not abandoned his people to their divisions and does not cease to lead them forward on their pilgrimage towards unity.

VIII.   Recommendations

This document suggests many initiatives that usefully might be taken by churches, episcopal conferences, NCCs and REOs. Two further recommendations, however, might stimulate the World Council of Churches and the Holy See to encourage Roman Catholic participation in ecumenical structures.

1. *Distribution of "Inspired by the Same Vision".* Its arguments deserve to be weighed by churches in each country and region and, if found persuasive, acted upon. Responses should be noted, so that "Inspired by the Same Vision" serves to stimulate discussion, not end it.

Recommendation:

That the Pontifical Council for Promoting Christian Unity and the World Council of Churches send this document to all NCCs, REOs, Eastern Catholic synods and Catholic episcopal conferences for study and comment, with the recommendation and encouragement that in those countries and regions where the Roman Catholic Church is not presently a member of the NCC or REO, a joint committee composed of members of the NCC, REO and bishops conference be formed which would have the responsibility to translate the document and distribute it to all NCC member churches and all Catholic bishops; and where appropriate, that they initiate a joint process of consultation among representatives of the NCC and bishops conference to examine the possibility of Catholic membership in an existing NCC or the formation of a new inclusive ecumenical body.

2. *Further consultation:* The Pontifical Council for Promoting Christian Unity and the World Council of Churches have sponsored three useful consultations on issues connected with NCCs – in 1971, 1986 and 1993. This report provides a timely occasion for another gathering. There is need for a new international consultation to bring together representatives of NCCs, REOs and episcopal conferences, especially from places where the Roman Catholic Church is not in membership.

Recommendation:

That the World Council of Churches and the Pontifical Council for Promoting Christian Unity be asked to co-sponsor a consultation of representatives of NCCs, REOs and episcopal conferences from places where the Roman Catholic Church is not in membership. The consultation should consider the document "Inspired by the Same Vision" and reflect on the experience others have gleaned regarding Catholic participation.

IX. Appendices

A. A SHORT BIBLIOGRAPHY

1. Thomas F. Best, "Councils of Churches: Local, National, Regional", http://www.wcc-coe.org/wcc/what/ecumenical/cc_e.html
2. World Council of Churches, "Church and Ecumenical Organizations", http://www.wcc-coe.org/wcc/links/church.html
3. Huibert van Beek, "Councils of Churches – a Discussion Starter", http://www.wcc-coe.org/wcc/who/damascus_06_e.html
4. Pontifical Council for Promoting Christian Unity, *Ecumenical Collaboration at the Regional, National, and Local Levels* (Vatican City, 1975).
5. Pontifical Council for Promoting Christian Unity, *The Ecumenical Dimension in the Formation of Those Engaged in Pastoral Work*, Vatican, 1995, §29. http://www.vatican.va/roman_curia/pontifical_councils/chrstuni/documents/
6. "Directory for the Application of Principles and Norms on Ecumenism", http://www.vatican.va/roman_curia/ pontifical_councils/chrstuni/documents/
7. Diane Kessler and Michael Kinnamon, *Councils of Churches and the Ecumenical Vision*, WCC Publications, 2000.

8. Jean-Marie Tillard, OP, "The Mission of the Councils of Churches", *The Ecumenical Review*, 45, 3, July 1993.
9. *Odyssey towards Unity: Foundations and Functions of Ecumenism and Conciliarism*, by Committee on Purposes and Goals of Ecumenism, Massachusetts Council of Churches, Boston MA, Mass. Council of Churches, Oct. 1977.
10. Thomas Michel, "Participation of the Roman Catholic Church in National Councils of Churches: An Historical Survey", *Jeevadhara* (Kottayam), July 2000.
11. *Charta Oecumenica*, Guidelines for the Growing Cooperation among the Churches in Europe, Geneva/St Gallen, 2001.

B. NCCs AND REOs WITH CATHOLIC MEMBERSHIP

Regional Ecumenical Organizations
Caribbean Conference of Churches
Middle East Conference of Churches
Pacific Conference of Churches

National Councils of Churches/Christian Councils

Africa: 14
Botswana (Botswana Christian Council)
Congo (Ecumenical Council of Christian Churches of Congo)
Gambia (Christian Council of The Gambia)
Lesotho (Christian Council of Lesotho)
Liberia (Liberian Council of Churches)
Madagascar (Council of Christian Churches in Madagascar)
Namibia (Council of Churches in Namibia)
Nigeria (Christian Council of Nigeria)
Sierra Leone (Council of Churches in Sierra Leone)
South Africa (South African Council of Churches)
Sudan (Sudan Council of Churches)
Swaziland (Council of Swaziland Churches)
Uganda (Uganda Joint Christian Council)
Zimbabwe (Zimbabwe Council of Churches), RC observer

Asia: 3
Australia (National Council of Churches in Australia)
Malaysia (Christian Federation of Malaysia)
Taiwan (National Council of Churches of Taiwan)

Caribbean: 12
Antigua (Antigua Christian Council)
Aruba (Aruba Council of Churches)
Bahamas (Bahamas Christian Council)
Barbados (Barbados Christian Council)
Belize (Belize Christian Council)
Curacao (Curacao Council of Churches)
Dominica (Dominica Christian Council)
Jamaica (Jamaica Council of Churches)

Montserrat (Montserrat Christian Council)
St Kitts/Nevis (St Kitts Christian Council)
St Vincent (St Vincent and the Grenadines Christian Council)
Trinidad and Tobago (Christian Council of Trinidad and Tobago)

Europe: 25
Austria (Council of Churches in Austria)
Belgium (Meeting of Christian Churches in Belgium)
Britain and Ireland (Churches Together in Britain and Ireland)
Croatia (Ecumenical Coordinating Committee of Churches in Croatia)
Czech Republic (Ecumenical Council of Churches in the Czech Republic),
   RC associate
Denmark (National Council of Churches in Denmark)
England (Churches Together in England)
Estonia (Estonian Council of Churches)
Finland (Finnish Ecumenical Council)
France (Council of Christian Churches in France)
Germany (Council of Christian Churches in Germany)
Hungary (Ecumenical Council of Churches in Hungary)
Ireland (Irish Council of Churches), RC observer
Ireland (Irish Inter-Church Meeting)
Isle of Man (Churches Together in Man)
Lithuania (National Council of Churches in Lithuania)
Malta (Malta Ecumenical Council)
Norway (Christian Council of Norway)
Netherlands (Council of Churches in the Netherlands)
Scotland (Action of Churches Together in Scotland)
Slovak Republic (Ecumenical Council of Churches in the Slovak Republic),
   RC observer
Slovenia (Council of Christian Churches in Slovenia)
Sweden (Christian Council of Sweden)
Switzerland (Council of Christian Churches in Switzerland)
Wales (Cytun – Churches Together in Wales)

North America: 1
Canada (Canadian Council of Churches)

Oceania: 10
American Samoa (National Council of Churches in American Samoa)
Cook Islands (Religious Advisory Council of the Cook Islands)
Fiji (Fiji Council of Churches)
Kiribati (Kiribati National Council of Churches)
Marshall Islands (Marshall Islands National Council of Churches of Christ)
Papua New Guinea (Papua New Guinea Council of Churches)
Samoa (Samoa Council of Churches)
Solomon Islands (Solomon Islands Christian Association)
Tonga (Tonga National Council of Churches)
Vanuatu (Vanuatu Christian Council)

South America: 5
   Argentina (Ecumenical Commission of Christian Churches in Argentina)
   Brazil (National Council of Christian Churches in Brazil)
   Guyana (Guyana Council of Churches)
   Surinam (Committee of Christian Churches – Surinam)
   Uruguay (Uruguay Council of Christian Churches)

C. LIST OF ABBREVIATIONS

AACC	All Africa Conference of Churches
ACC	Australian Council of Churches
ARCIC	Anglican-Roman Catholic International Commission
CCA	Christian Conference of Asia
CCANZ	Conference of Churches, Aotearoa-New Zealand
CCC	Caribbean Conference of Churches
CCEE	Consilium Conferentiarum Episcoporum Europae
CEC	Conference of European Churches
CECEF	Conseil d'Églises chrétiennes en France (Council of Christian Churches in France)
CELAM	Latin American Episcopal Conference
CLAI	Consejo Latinoamericano de Iglesias (Latin American Council of Churches)
CTBI	Churches Together in Britain and Ireland
CUV	*Towards a Common Understanding and Vision of the World Council of Churches*
DAP	*Directory for the Application of Principles and Norms on Ecumenism*
EC	*Ecumenical Collaboration at the Regional, National, and Local Levels*
FABC	Federation of Asian Bishops Conferences
ICC	Irish Council of Churches
LG	*Lumen Gentium* (Vatican Council II Constitution on the Church)
MECC	Middle East Council of Churches
NCC	National Council of Churches
NCCA	National Council of Churches in Australia
REO	Regional Ecumenical Organization
PCC	Pacific Conference of Churches
PCPCU	Pontifical Council for Promoting Christian Unity
SECAM	Symposium of Episcopal Conferences of Africa and Madagascar
UR	*Unitatis Redintegratio* (Vatican Council II Decree on Ecumenism)
YMCA	Young Men's Christian Association
WCC	World Council of Churches

NOTE

¹ This document sometimes uses the term "Catholic Church" in preference to "Roman Catholic Church." In some regional and national ecumenical organizations, it is the wider "Catholic" family that is represented; this situation may be reflected in the constitutions of some national and regional councils of churches with use of the term "Catholic."

Glossary of Abbreviations

ACT	Action by Churches Together
BEM	*Baptism Eucharist Ministry*
CCIA	Commission of the Churches on International Affairs
CCEE	Council of European Bishops Conferences
CEC	Conference of European Churches
CEP	Congregation for the Evangelization of Peoples
CWME	Commission on World Mission and Evangelism
CWCs	Christian World Communions
CUV	*Common Understanding and Vision of the WCC*
DOV	Decade to Overcome Violence
EEF	Education and Ecumenical Formation
ETE	Ecumenical Theological Education
ICMC	International Catholic Migration Commission
IRRD	WCC Office on Interreligious Relations and Dialogue
IUSG	International Union of Superiors General
JRS	Jesuit Refugee Services
JWG	Joint Working Group
LG	*Lumen Gentium*
MECC	Middle East Council of Churches
NCCs	National Councils of Churches
NGOs	Non-Governmental Organisations
NMI	*Novo Millennio Ineunte*
PCID	Pontifical Council for Interreligious Dialogue
PCJP	Pontifical Council for Justice and Peace
PCPCU	Pontifical Council for Promoting Christian Unity
RC	Roman Catholic
RCC	Roman Catholic Church
REOs	Regional Ecumenical Organizations
SEDOS	Servizio di Documentazione e Studi

TMA	*Tertio Millennio Adveniente*
UN	United Nations
UNHCR	United Nations High Commissioner for Refugees
UR	*Unitatis Redintegratio*
USG	Union of Superiors General
WCC	World Council of Churches

Cet ouvrage a été achevé d'imprimer en mai 2005
dans les ateliers de Normandie Roto Impression s.a.s.
61250 Lonrai (Orne)
N° d'impression : 05-1184
Dépôt légal : mai 2005

Imprimé en France